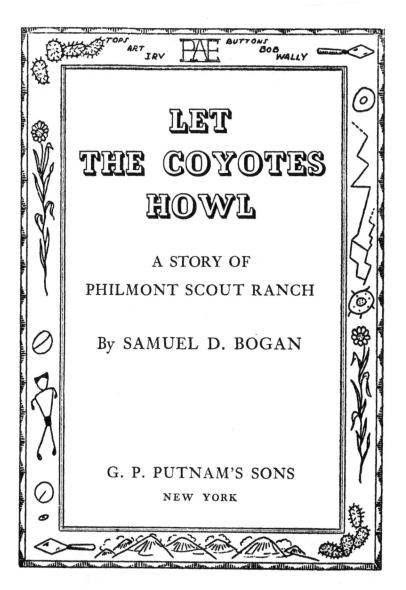

LET THE COYOTES HOWL

A STORY OF PHILMONT SCOUT RANCH

By SAMUEL D. BOGAN

G. P. PUTNAM'S SONS

NEW YORK

To

WAITE PHILLIPS

*whose faith in the American boy
brought us, at last, to
The Shining Mountains*

ACKNOWLEDGMENTS

I am deeply obliged to the Boy Scouts of America for sanction and approval of explorations within the great Philmont Ranch properties of the organization, and to the archaeological staff of the Peabody Museum at Yale University for invaluable advice and assistance.

My greatest obligation will always remain with the youthful members of the expedition. They have been willing to have the record stand as it happened, and the use of their personal diaries has been a valuable check against my own observations. I should like to introduce them: Bob is Robert Butler, Tops is Aubrey Davies, Art is Arthur Eade, Jr., Wally is Wallace Rubin, Buttons is Norman Shemitz, and Irv is Irving Versoy. The combination is dynamite or inspiration, depending somewhat upon the mood of the moment.

Foreword

THIS day-by-day narrative of events on a scout expedition will interest every ex-scout by reviving memories of his own experiences and his fondest daydreams. The contemporary scout will find it fascinating as proof that his own hopes are not beyond realization. That the members of this party chose an archaeological objective is not vital, for had they been interested in a survey of insect life, small rodents, reptiles, birds, or even wild plants, their story would have been equally interesting. In fact, many other objectives could be chosen, all equally promising, such as making a topographical map, a geological survey, or a study of stream and wind erosion. Finally, a historical program could be devised, such as following the trail of De Soto, part of the trail of Lewis and Clark, or the path of prairie schooners along the Old Platte Trail.

The scout leader upon whom the success of such an excursion depends will find this volume a first-class reference. He can read between the lines, sensing the daily problems of personality adjustment arising in the camp. The idea of hinting that each boy keep his own diary is more important than it may seem. Further, the leader shows a fine hand in finding the right pair for each tent and in arranging the program so that each boy can exploit his preferred skill to best advantage. Teamwork is seldom real if each technical skill is everybody's business. Finally, it is easy to overlook the necessity for the preliminary study, planning, and practice which is needed to make teamwork effective enough to realize the full objectives of such an excursion.

This book reminded the writer of the important contribution made to scouting by the late B. Talbot B. Hyde—"Uncle Benny," as he was affectionately called by the boys who knew him. How he would have enjoyed reading it! In the days when scout summer camps were still an experiment, Mr. Hyde saw in them opportunities to lead boys in the study of nature, each according to his own inclination. Every plant, every rock, every living thing was to Hyde worthy of study. When a boy came to him with a question, his usual attitude was, "I know little or nothing about it, but I'm sure that you and I can find out if we go about it in the right way." He was firm in the faith that no problem in natural history is too "high and mighty" to be above the comprehension of his boys if reduced to concrete situations and clear statements. His method might be reduced to the homely statement that "the best education results when the individual unconsciously educates himself." He believed that the need for accuracy of observation and precision in logic would appeal to the boy and inspire him to value the dignity and integrity of the truth. This is the character of *Let the Coyotes Howl*.

The value of the scout organization is not solely in the routine of the troops, nor in the ideal of "a good turn daily." It flowers best in the subtle companionship between boy and leader, seeking comprehension of the world in which we live. Educators recognize several cardinal objectives in education, among which are:

a) the appreciation of aesthetic materials, as in art, music, and literature;
b) a wider appreciation of the world in which we live, or nature;
c) an appreciation of the culture in which we live, or the human environment.

The objectives we have just enumerated coincide closely with the prime purposes of the Boy Scout organization. Thus the procedure of a "hike" is directed particularly at the appreciation of nature, at taking the boy out of doors where he may experience some of the closeness to nature enjoyed by our primitive ancestors; but in addition it brings to bear upon what the scout observes, the superior knowledge to be found in our best books. So far, good understandable books dealing with such experiences are almost nonexistent. We hope this pioneer volume will encourage more boy leaders to make similar contributions by furnishing other specific examples of what is meant by "standing face to face with nature."

CLARK WISSLER
Curator Emeritus, Department of
Anthropology,
The American Museum of Natural History;
Member at Large, National Council,
Boy Scouts of America

LIST OF ILLUSTRATIONS

(Illustrations between pages 80-81)

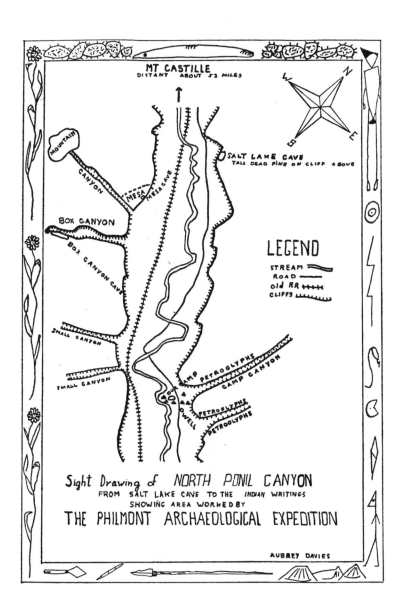

Sight Drawing of *NORTH PONIL CANYON*
FROM SALT LAKE CAVE TO THE *INDIAN* WRITINGS
SHOWING AREA WORKED BY
THE PHILMONT ARCHAEOLOGICAL EXPEDITION

AUBREY DAVIES

The First Chapter

O brightest planets and fixed stars,
   Loveliest company of sky!
Grant us to flash like meteors,
   One flaming light before we die.

Sunday, August 17

WEATHER: Fair at dawn, cloudy later with scattered thunder showers.

CONDITION of Party: Animated.

I sat up in my sleeping bag to see the dawn come flowing from the fountain of the rising sun. It washed the sky and plain in a pearl-like glow and enveloped us, at last, in a warm wave of rose.

Tops, standing between me and the sun, was a lone figure on the vast horizon. We had slept on a plain so level that the sun seemed to rise at our feet and the grasses to stretch away like a sea out of which small birds rose like flying fish. Drops of dew reflected the morning and, when we moved, rolled down our sleeping bags in small streams of amber.

During the night a coyote had howled across the plain. In a sense we were kindred with him, keeping the same company of stars and meteors; yet, in his cunning, he could not trust us. He is so wild, and we are so far removed from nature, that we can do little better than pay each other the compliment of indifference.

Last night, as we set up camp, we made a wide circle of grass rope around our sleeping bags, thus, in the tradition of the West, erecting a barrier against the rattlesnakes which might otherwise have come to bed with us. This idea, which has found its way into the folklore of the West, may be only a superstition, but my young

2

campers were serious enough about it. Wally inspected the rope with special care and moved his sleeping bag as near the center of the charmed circle as he could.

We lay on our backs and looked far away into the sky. There was no roof over us and the stars seemed very near. There were many meteors. Listening to their conversation, I sensed in my companions the deep unrest of youth, the uneasy awe of the unknown.

"What is it all about?" they inquired.

"No one can tell," I answered, "but it is better to enjoy it than to worry about it."

Our home roof sometimes cuts us off from the part of heaven which is most sure, the open and starry sky. The wideness of the night makes for wider thoughts. The day is brighter but we do not see so far. Someday an architect will devise a roof that can be rolled aside on clear nights, by the touch of a button, perhaps, and we shall have our universe whenever the skies are clear.

"No rattlesnakes," reported Buttons as he looked carefully into his shoes before putting them on.

"Huh, you don't have to worry," retorted Irv. "They would be dead if they had crawled in there."

"Well, anyway," Buttons replied, "I slept good in spite of the hardiness of the ground."

"Hardiness," snorted Irv, "Buttons has an adjustable vocabulary."

After two thousand miles of travel we have become expert in making and breaking camp. My six scouts can roll their packs, load our station wagon, and be ready to travel in a few minutes. This day seemed especially important, as we are scheduled to reach our destination, Philmont Scout Ranch, near Cimarron, New Mexico, where we are commissioned to conduct an archaeological exploration.

In breaking camp each member of the party makes his own pack and places it in a specified position for loading. Then everyone pitches in on the tents. Packing completed, Tops and Irv make the tentage and blanket rolls fast on the car roof while Bob and Art stow the rest of the equipment inside. Meanwhile Buttons has been cleaning the inside of the wagon with a whisk broom and Wally wiping off the outside and polishing the windows, windshield, and headlights. All of which gives me about ten minutes to check the route and chart our course for the day.

Since it is not considered good ethics for any one of the boys to establish himself until all are ready, I make a last-minute inspection of men and equipment, give the word, and then watch them trip over each other in a rush for favored positions. Within a few seconds they settle down and I see a constellation of faces in the rear-vision mirror. It is an animated pattern, hardly one of fixed stars, but it means all present and accounted for. The starter grinds, the motor hums, and we flow out into the current of a new day.

During the morning we drove the rough and winding road to the top of El Capulin. This extinct volcano stands, a lonesome hulk of earth, far apart from the neighboring mountains. But Capulin's best glory is past, vanished in the smoke of her dead fires. At the summit we thought less of El Capulin, more of the great sweep of world before us, the unending plains south and eastward, the mountains north and westward. There is

4

enough land to satisfy a Caesar in this *Lebensraum* of the hawk and the hare.

El Capulin's elderly caretaker, or ranger, spoke eloquently on behalf of his heap of lava, and we sensed that he really loved his cindered mountain. Impressed, the boys explored the crater carefully and several of them stored souvenir cinders in their pockets. Art, who disdained to do this, confided to me that "After all, it's just dirt."

We stopped to look for horned toads and found black widow spiders, *Lactrodectus mactans*, instead. Their color scheme of glossy black with the bright orange hourglass under the abdomen is dramatic enough to be dangerous.

"The hourglass," said Irv, "is to remind you that your time has come if you fool with one."

She ("the female of the species is more deadly than the male") is about the size of an old-fashioned buckshot with legs on it. For her size she may be the most poisonous creature known to man. The male is hardly a fourth as large and may be considered dangerous chiefly because he is a courageous lover. He perpetuates the species at the risk of his life, for the widow is cannibalistic and may eat him on only slight provocation.

The thread from which she spins her web is fluid within the body and hardens on contact with the air. It is reputed to be stronger than steel wire of the same diameter.

A creature to be feared by man, the widow is just another morsel to some of the birds who take her down as you might a dash of piccalilli.

We arrived at Philmont at two-thirty in the afternoon

5

and, after traveling for about five miles over a rough and boulder-strewn road, reached our destination at Five Points at three o'clock.

We were billeted in the unfinished Scouters' Lodge west of the Trading Post and found it to our liking. Several native workmen were there and we struck up an acquaintance. They were skilled artisans, proud of their work. Their foreman was a minister and they reserved their lustiest tales for moments when he was out of hearing. The Lodge, built of native pine and spruce logs, was tight, strong, and pleasing to look at. The boys considered it a distinction to be the first campers to occupy it.

After a check by the doctor we reported to the main lodge for supper. This building is constructed of imported logs and, though sturdy, is less appealing to the eye than our living quarters. The pale Oregon logs seem out of place but we were informed it had been less expensive to transport them than to cut timbers from the native hills. This is a sad habit, to sacrifice beauty to the lowest bidder, and, in the long pull, may not be a true economy.

Our meal included pinto beans, lye hominy, and bacon cut in thick slabs from the side of the pork. The bacon we particularly liked in contrast to the thin, machine-sliced stuff to which we were accustomed. Here was meat that would stick to the ribs, standing on its own merits of body and savor, and more than a mere flavoring for eggs.

The lye hominy was new to Buttons who looked at it with a suspicious eye.

"It looks like beans cooked in flour," he remarked,

6

and the knowledge that it was hulled corn prepared by saturating the grain in lye did not enhance his opinion of the bland dish.

At the lodge we ran into a couple of fellows who had just come in from fishing. They had had good luck, so they did most of the talking. There are a number of fine streams within the ranch which I should like to try. But fishing and archaeology do not mix. The first requires a sense of leisure and the latter diligence.

A man's fishing days should begin at about age seven, with the lowly angleworm for bait. He should learn to bait his own hook from the beginning and, if fortunate, have a fishing companion not much older than himself.

When I was twelve or so, and at the height of my catfishing days, I fished with Wilbur, the small son of our Negro washwoman, down in the deep South. He taught me the importance of spitting on my hook, and of wearing a bit of asafoetida around my neck for good luck; and even though my family vetoed this latter charm, I found that rubbing my hook on Wilbur's neckpiece was powerful medicine. Wilbur never worried about the fish biting.

"The fishes got all day, and so have I," was his answer to my impatience.

A man should have two hobbies, one of the body and one of the mind. The first should be manual or athletic, like hiking, gardening, carpentry, or painting; and the second should be intellectual, as natural history, chemistry, poetry, or research. If possible both should be creative, and neither should relate to the manner in which one earns a living. The person who tells you that

7

his work is his hobby is unimaginative, and even he would probably do his work better after a bit of a change.

I like fishing because, as a contemplative hobby, it is in a class by itself.

Before we went to sleep there was talk of right and wrong. It is an amazing world in which we live two lives, one of the mind and spirit within ourselves, and one in obedience to the law of the pack. We must be great in the first in order to reconcile it with the second, to understand that when the pack runs the individual cannot stay, yet may carry with him, wherever he goes, something of the finer life he lives within himself.

There is no perfection in the mind. We do not acknowledge within ourselves as much of the beautiful as we see in one small flower, or in one clear crystal of geometric snow.

The Second Chapter

I saw the flag of America flying and had no
  proper words to tell of it.
I could never say enough in praise of my
  land without new words.
Where are the splendid rhymes and the most
  ringing syllables?
Where are the affectionate words that shine
  like constellations on a page?
Is any voice richer than the song of the
  thrush at twilight?
Has the wind a new sound, or the thunder
  a music to be spoken?
Tell me which river has language more lasting than the ripples on its shore.
Is there a mighty echo in the mountains
  which can speak?

Dear Native Land! Mother America!
Since I do not have new words to praise you,
I will tread lightly in my ways
That I may caress you in every step I take.

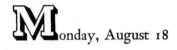

Monday, August 18

WEATHER: Fair and cool at dawn. Showers in the late afternoon.

CONDITION of Party: Curious.

"Dawn, the rosy-fingered," I quoted to Irv as the first light filtered through our lodge windows. Buttons, emerging sleepy-eyed from his cocoon-shaped sleeping bag, stretched and yawned gutturally.

"This is like getting up in the middle of the night," he complained.

"And thar's ice in them hills," shouted Bob, making a dash for the blaze of wood scraps and shavings which Tops had lighted in the fireplace.

"Breakfast at six-fifteen!" groaned Wally. "My folks will never believe I made it."

Meanwhile Art had dressed quietly and was seated on his cot writing a postcard home. His father, he tells me, is an exceptional man, and I mentally marked the relationship a success, as I had already been privately informed by the father that Art is an exceptional lad.

We walked to breakfast in a penetrating mist and ate our food by lantern light. The lodge, having been designed, I suspect, in an office in New York, is short on windows. It might serve well enough on a hilltop, but nestling beneath these towering mountains, it will remain dark on the brightest days. The architect's sketches, no doubt, were beautiful, with Lombardy poplar trees spaced in all the most appropriate places.

Wally and Buttons raised the flag. I saw them stand and watch it unfurl, and I thought they were going to salute but they did not. Wally raised his hand in the gesture one uses in waving to a friend, and Buttons drew a deep breath before he turned away. Each in his own way had paid tribute to the flag, revealing not a mere formal respect but an abiding affection.

The base camp where we are situated is known as "Five Points." It is located in a canyon between rugged mountains, with a fine stream, normally running muddy, meandering through. The sandstone ledges in the canyon walls show evidences of early Indians, including the remains of a dry wall, the residue from ancient fires, and, on top of the cliff northwest of the Lodge, a circular stone arrangement about twenty feet in diameter which Camp Director B. B. Dawson describes as a tepee circle. We made a small test dig in its center but did not find anything which we could positively identify as of Indian origin. We did find authentic flint chippings on the surface near by.

Meanwhile, a party of explorer scouts from Salt Lake City returned from North Ponil Canyon with reports of a cave, and with the well-charred remains of a cooking pot, all in sherds, but seemingly enough to reconstruct. They also brought from the same site a well-graded batch of feathers, probably magpie, but poorly preserved because of their great age.

The Salt Lake boys were a husky and a devout lot who came in from their long hike singing. They joined us in the Lodge for lunch. I have met Mormons before and have been impressed by their singular devotion.

Theirs is a new and vigorous church and its young men do not have to look beyond their own grandfathers or great-uncles to find the heroes and martyrs of their faith. Like Voltaire's Quakers, they stand to surprise the world by actually behaving like Christians.

Several other parties of scouts are in the valley and during the afternoon I hiked down to see their encampments. They had everything from pup tents (which rate about zero as camping equipment) to eight-man wall tents. One party had an Indian tepee which must have been for atmosphere. I do not think it could have been for comfort.

At one point a scout from Louisiana was trying to teach one of the ranch hands how to spin a rope. He twirled it in either hand, jumping in and out of the swinging circle while alternately raising and lowering it over his head and around his body.

The admiring cowboy admitted that his own technique was better for lassoing stumps.

"Son," he said, "you ought to stick around for the Labor Day Rodeo. I reckon you might win a prize."

"Rodeo is no place for me," the boy replied. "I belong on *terra firma* unless you've got a rubber-tired horse."

The cook at the Lodge is known to the boys as Max the Mexican. Tops described him to me as mysterious, almost sinister. As I watched Max move silently about his work, I observed that he grinned widely when anyone caught his eye, but said little, and I guessed he was using that wide smile in lieu of his uncertain English. This evening, since he is billeted near by, he stopped at our quarters and was quietly sociable for a while.

"It's funny," Tops said afterward, "but Max is a pretty good fellow once you know him."

"Yeah," said Irv, "it usually turns out that way."

We are known as the Philmont Archaeological Expedition, * and the boys are enjoying a mild distinction. As members of this expedition, they consider themselves something more than ordinary campers. They are embryonic scientists and, as they climb the cliffs with their measuring implements, tools, cameras, and record books, they are not unimpressive. Trained to a light pack, they do not carry unnecessary paraphernalia. There is pride in their walk and, indeed, they have earned the right to flaunt their banners just a little.

Through the weeks and months before leaving New Haven they worked hard to prepare themselves. Wally, our photographer, underwent a long and careful apprenticeship under a professional in order to earn his place, while Buttons, Bob, and Art spent hours at the Peabody Museum at Yale University under the kind tutelage of Alexis Praus. Tops and Irv studied minerals and surveying. All attended lectures and field trips. Now, over two thousand miles from home, in the canyons of northeastern New Mexico, they have what they wanted most: a chance to test their learning and try their skill. "In traveling," said Ben Johnson, "a man must carry knowledge with him if he would bring home knowledge," and in the spirit of the scout motto we have tried to "Be prepared."

* Actually we were known as the *Philturn Archaeological Expedition*, as our visit took place several months before the name of this great camp was changed to the Philmont Scout Ranch. We changed the name of our expedition in order to avoid misunderstanding.

I anticipate that this will be a journal of plain deeds and thoughts in which no one is killed, or accused unjustly, or outwitted by an enemy. There is a certain satisfaction in the ordinary, and we propose to enjoy it without stint. Most adventures are chores in the having, however exciting they may be in the telling.

The Third Chapter

These are my lads and I would serve them well
Before they lose the growing time of youth.
I wish I knew exactly what to tell ...
Only the ignorant are sure of truth.

Tuesday, August 19

WEATHER: Fair, temperature at 7 A.M. 60° F.

CONDITION of Party: Sprinkled with impatience.

Archaeological digging must be done with a certain reverence. Carelessness may blot out whole pages of discovery; hurry may blur the clarity of others. The eye must be vigilant and the mind inquisitive with the realization that one is not seeking things so much as knowledge. A beautiful artifact, unrelated to the exact place and facts of its discovery, may lose its entire significance.

As you dig, unmindful of aching back and blistered palms, you try to re-create the life and customs of an ancient people. Sometimes you can almost see them before your eyes, and you try to think the thoughts that may have been theirs. You look out upon the same timeless contours, and touch with your hands the walls that they once knew, running your fingers through deposits of soot from their ancient fires. You hear the same bird song and water trickle, taste a similar pure and zestful air, feeling, as Roy Chapman Andrews once said, that "The study of the past is warm with life," and that from this warmth one may still find animation enough to illumine some unrecorded page in the history of man.

We staked out the low overhanging cave in the rear of the Trading Post and made two test digs to sterile

16

soil. (Sterile soil is that which is of the original earth and which remains undisturbed by animal or vegetable detritus.) We also made an uneventful test in the caves northwest of the Lodge adjacent to the dry wall. I did not expect anything in particular from these sites, but was glad to give my crew some preliminary practice in excavation.

The procedure is not complicated. First, the site is staked out, usually in six-foot squares, which are lettered and cross-numbered so that each is easily identified in the record. Digging is done with caution lest important evidence be destroyed. One is likely to use a trowel more than pick or shovel, and to remove the soil in horizontal layers.

The location of each important specimen or artifact is plotted on a graph, with its position and depth carefully noted. The material found in each section or square is then kept in a separate sack or container. Important finds may be catalogued on the spot, and are often individually wrapped and packed.

The camera is an essential tool, and saves many pages of description. Wally is prepared to give us proof copies of all important pictures the same day they are taken.

Theoretically, a good archaeologist can put his site together again after it has been excavated. We plan to be careful, but we hope we are not asked to do this.

Excepting the trowels, which are basic, our favorite tools are a geologist's pick, designed by Professor Marsh of Yale, and a florist's spade. The pick is of rolled steel with a fine point on one end and a sharp cutting edge on the other, with a strong hickory handle about twenty-four inches long. This tool is especially useful in cutting and removing roots, and in loosening stones. I rate it as the best single implement in our equipment.

The florist's spade is strongly made and capable of hard wear, but its best feature is the combination of small blade with long handle. The blade, or shovel, is about the size of any ordinary trench shovel, while the handle is full length. It handles well and has a way of doing what we intend instead of slicing to the right or hooking to the left.

We did not attempt a painstaking archaeological survey of Five Points. The signs found there seemed, with few exceptions, to indicate transient Indians who may have hunted or traveled through.

Mr. Dawson, the camp director, exhibited some specimens which he had accumulated. These included a number of potsherds, one of them black on white pueblo, two pairs of yucca sandals, one round-toed and one square-toed, and a few arrowheads.

Just now we are impatient. Our time is limited and, to our distress, the supplies we shipped did not arrive in Cimarron on the Saturday train. The next train was due today (Tuesday) and, in our anxiety, we decided to meet it. The boys' eyes sparkled when they saw our stuff actually unloaded, as this means we shall be able to leave for location tomorrow.

We took time for a little shopping. For the boys this consisted mainly of chocolate bars, chewing gum, and camera film. I checked our first-aid kit and stocked up on iodine, bandages, and rubbing alcohol.

Wally wanted the baseball scores so he took a newspaper from the stand, turned to the sports page, and, after getting the information desired, returned the paper to the stand.

"Suppose you pay for the paper, Wally," I suggested.

"I don't want it, Chief. I'm through with it."

"But the paper is merchandise. You haven't any more right to use it without paying than you have to any other item in the store."

"But, Chief ..."

"Suppose you pay for it, Wally."

"Sure, Chief."

Paying the nickel, he put the paper in his pocket.

"I'm going to read the rest of it back in camp," he explained. "I only got two cents' worth. I've got to read it all the way through to get my nickel's worth."

I hoped he might forget the incident and remember the principle.

Bob, impressed with the natives, described them in his diary:

"Men squatted along the sidewalks with their backs to the store fronts. Their faces were bronzed by the sun and wind, the kind of men that are numerous in the Southwest. I could not look into those steely light-blue eyes for long. They made me feel like a dude with my fair skin and hardly soiled dungarees. This is the true West which the world of the fine arts, night clubs, and high society has not changed. But, in spite of my different clothes, they call me a brother. We are all Americans."

Facing the main street of Cimarron there is a primitive statue of one Lucien B. Maxwell sitting, gun in hand, through all weathers. It does not rain often enough to wash him away although the statue is made of adobe-like material. It was constructed by an artist of unintelligible initials and we do not think it flatters the figure it is supposed to represent. It would be our guess that if Mr. Maxwell has a grave to turn over in, it is probably the busiest in all New Mexico.

After supper we returned to our quarters and the boys sat on their cots talking intimately. They had traveled far, seen many cities and the wide wilderness, and they had learned to work and to camp together. In quiet moments they shared a store of hidden knowledge: the power of airplanes, the mystery of girls, or man's place in the great but conquerable world.

I have yet to read a technical book about boys that does them justice. Tom Sawyer and Huckleberry Finn are true. Penrod is real. But technical books about boys are pies made of sawdust. Show me an expert on boys, and I will pass by with my fishing rod and his "group" will desert him to follow me and be my "gang." We do not need experts, but men acquainted with life to lead our sons.

The world is full of so-called scholars riding their specialties, but true scholarship is broader than professional efficiency. It can never be just music, or just bones, or just anything. It must be wider than an acre of knowledge fenced in with the barbed wire of specialization. We may scorn the "jack of all trades, master of none," but we will one day revere the wise man who can be a jack of all trades and master of *one*.

The Fourth Chapter

The dawn is far away,
And the tired day
Rests on night's shoulders.
In the young twilight,
Sleep has wings tonight;
The campfire smolders.

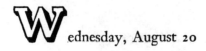

Wednesday, August 20

WEATHER: Fair during the morning, showers in the late afternoon.

CONDITION of Party: Weary.

Darwin, in the *Voyage of the Beagle*, would have taken ten pages to narrate the activities of our morning, no doubt agitating every insect on the trail, but the day has been too much for me, and I am ready for bed.

We were up at five-thirty, breakfasted at six-fifteen, and by nine o'clock had loaded our chuck wagon and sent Billy Wetsel, the native cowboy assigned to us, on his way to location in North Ponil Canyon, with Wally as passenger. Completing our arrangements at Base Camp, and finding that no horses were available, we slung our packs on our backs and hiked over the mountain, eating our lunch on a high and windy summit.

Buttons described the hike:

"The scenery, new and exciting, was breath-taking. The mountains made me feel insignificant as we trudged along, but I felt better when Chief stocked us with chocolate bars for extra energy."

Buttons, who stands about five feet in his stockings, is a bit short for his age. Irv teases him by yelling, "Stand up, Buttons!" when he is already on his feet. These taunts have no apparent effect, Buttons remaining confident enough in his other qualities. His slight deficiency in stature is more than offset by his natural grace. His black hair glistens like a magazine advertisement, and he has brought vaseline oil to the wilderness to keep it shining.

Reaching our camp site in the early afternoon, we found a three-days-dead muskrat in the well, and much litter of careless camping on the ground. We immediately organized to bring order out of this chaos; Billy setting up his chuck wagon and outdoor kitchen, Tops and Irv digging a garbage pit six feet long, four feet deep, and two feet wide, Art and Bob digging a latrine, and Wally and Buttons picking up tin cans and other remnants, with which they filled half of the new garbage pit, much to the distress of Tops and Irv, who had dug it with three weeks' camping in mind.

All joined hands to erect six wall tents, six by ten feet, located without attempt at symmetry but to take advantage of the best terrain. This was a race against an approaching shower which we partially lost, but we had all the tents pitched but two when the rain struck. Dry and secure, we were glad to rest in the snug shelter of our new quarters.

"This rain," said Art, "does not worry me. My pack is dry, and I have company."

"It has accomplished what nothing else could," Irv remarked dryly. "It has made Chief give us a rest."

We observed on our hike that the dominant trees on the mountain are yellow pine, scrub oak, juniper, Oregon fir (called spruce locally), and pinyon. In the valleys the cottonwood poplars and willows predominate, while the quaking aspen grows in clumps along the canyon walls.

The small nut from the pinyon tree is now a commercial crop, known in Eastern markets as the Indian nut. It has always been an important item in the diet of the Indians of this area. After a moving picture in one of the small New Mexican towns where the Indians are numerous, the aisles are often littered with the shells. We sampled the nuts and found that they have an oily, resinous flavor with a cool, aromatic overtone. The caloric content must be high, for a few are enough to dull the appetite. They taste best with a little salt.

On the canyon floors the most characteristic growth is that "eagle of flowers," the wild sunflower, and the rank jimson weed. "Careless weed" was also pointed out by our cowboy. All are luxuriant this year because of the rainiest season in a long time.

We worked until dark, when Billy called us to an excellent meal of fried ham, sweet potatoes with ham gravy, mixed vegetables, bread, butter, tea, and sliced peaches; a remarkable performance, considering the difficulties of getting camp started.

After supper Tops and Irv joined me for a council of war, and the others joined us later for discussion and assignments. Everybody was glad to retire early, although not without a fire and a story. Now at nine o'clock they are all asleep, and the sound of my typewriter competes only with the ripple of the stream and the cracklings of the forest night, for there is no wind.

I have been watching our cowboy closely during the day with a natural anxiousness. Relationships in a camp as small and intimate as ours may easily be upset by a discordant personality. But my fears are allayed. We are going to like Billy.

I feel guilty every time I think of that *Beagle*, but I am going to bed. Darwin has been cussed by better men than I, and for different reasons.

The Fifth Chapter

PHILMONT CAMPING SONG (Tune: "Red River Valley")

Oh, the rivers are never too wide,
  And the mountains are never too high,
For the good scouts who hike at my side
  In the land where the coyotes cry.

We will climb to the top of the world,
  We will drink from the clouds in the sky,
As our banners are proudly unfurled,
  On the heights where the thunder birds fly.

We will sing all the best melodies,
  And tell stories of yore by the fire;
We'll be happy and free as the breeze,
  Having all that our hearts desire.

Thursday, August 21

WEATHER: Fair in the morning. Showers in the afternoon.

CONDITION of Party: Calm.

We had breakfast late, seven-fifteen instead of six-fifteen. Hereafter, on location, we plan to breakfast at seven, lunch at noon, and have supper at six o'clock.

Billy's culinary ability is now established beyond question. This morning we had hot oatmeal, fresh sausage, fried eggs, hot coffee, and marvelous light rolls which were cooked in a Dutch oven and served piping hot with butter and strawberry jam. Irv said there should be a law against it, presumably because one is tempted to eat enough for three or four.

Our chuck wagon is identical with those used by the cowboys. It is so constructed that the chuck box, containing about a dozen compartments of various sizes, fits exactly into the last quarter of the wagon body. Its cover lets down to form a table which is easily adjusted to level position by means of a hinged leg. It takes Billy ten or fifteen minutes to unhitch the horses, open the chuck box, and be ready to prepare a meal in the open.

Following breakfast we continued our task of getting camp in order. We feel that this must be done right, as we are to remain here for some time. Bob, Buttons, and Irv continued policing the grounds, and made preparations to set up a canvas fly over our mess table. Mean-

26

while Tops and Art built a washstand with two legs lower than the others, a deficiency which they excused with the explanation that the spilled water would run off more naturally.

I asked Wally to make a path through the weeds to the latrine.

"Why?" he asked.

"Because," I replied, "at such a time no one wants to stop and apologize to a sunflower."

By midmorning our chores were done and we set out confidently for the cave in which the Salt Lake City scouts had discovered the potsherds and feathers. Working from the known toward the unknown, we had decided that this would be a good place to start. All morning we climbed and puffed and panted, peering into countless crevices and working along many a precarious cliff in search of the cave.

The landmarks emphasized by the Salt Lake City boys —an abrupt bend in the river and a tall dead pine on the cliff above—had sounded clear enough, but in the actual search we found the river a series of more or less abrupt bends with tall pines in all sorts of inconvenient places along the canyon walls. This delayed the discovery of Salt Lake Cave, as we have named it, until early afternoon.

Bob recorded the event in his diary:

"After a lot of exploring, Tops, Irv, Buttons, Wally, and I rendezvoused on the rim of the canyon, wondering what to do next. Then Tops lit off to find Chief who had last been seen about three-quarters of a mile to the northwest. We continued our search for the cave without success. This was discouraging. We wished to establish contact with Chief for further instructions but he was nowhere to be seen.

"Half an hour later we suddenly spied Tops and Chief silhouetted against the lowering clouds. We picked up our gear and high-tailed it toward the point where they had been. A few drops of rain came down to hurry us on, but when we puffed up to the spot where we had seen them, they had disappeared. The earth had swallowed them up.

"After more searching I found a path leading down through a fissure in the rim. We followed it down and suddenly there sat Tops and Chief in a beautiful little cave. We hastily opened our canteens and swallowed all the water we had left. Salt Lake Cave had been discovered. We had descended by the very trail the Indians must have used."

We waited out a series of showers in the cave, spending the time surface hunting. Wally found a fine potsherd and Art a clear obsidian chip. This afternoon, weather permitting, we will return to stake out the cave and begin a methodical excavation.

Salt Lake Cave is about a mile south of our camp on the northeast wall of the canyon and high in the cliffs, so we will have to work to get to it. Returning to camp a few minutes ago, after the showers, we had to contend with slippery rocks on the mountain and rich, slimy mud in the valley.

In the small canyon to the rear of our camp Billy has his horses, Dan and Prince, tethered while he works on a temporary corral for them. He has more fun, he says, feeding and caring for them, than in pouring gas into his flivver.

28

"The trouble with one of them gas buggies," he added, "is that they have no sentiment. They will let you down without no warnin', and they are worse than supportin' another member of the family."

On the walls of this same small canyon, and about one hundred feet from its mouth, are some Indian writings, or petroglyphs. Some of them have been marked over with chalk, and the location otherwise marred by notoriety-seeking visitors who have left their unimportant names beside the bold incisions of the nameless hunters of the past. Our site, known as Indian Writings, takes its name from these and adjacent petroglyphs.

The day continued wet with intermittent showers, so we did not return to the cave. Starting out after lunch with the intention of exploring some of the near-by cliffs, Irv and I climbed higher and higher until we reached the crest of the mountain northeast.

Sharp gusts of wind needled our faces with fine rain as we hiked in a penetrating chill. There was something elemental and primitive about it, and we liked it. To shrink from nature less, and brace one's self to meet her more squarely, is to discover in the cold wind and the rain not hardship but exhilarating joy.

Irv, who had been sheltered all his life, pitted his strength against the mountain and the weather with a gleam of uninhibited pleasure in his eye. There was no one to tell him to put on his rubbers, or not to get his hair wet, or to come in out of the rain. His lilting step was sure. When, at the summit, the clouds broke away and three impressive mountain ranges swung into view, we seemed almost to hold them in our hands. Irv turned to me wordless, but the radiance in his face was eloquent.

29

We returned through the small canyon which leads into camp by way of Billy's new corral, exploring the ledges along the way. The cliffs are composed of exceedingly loose, fine-grained material. It is treacherous climbing, and I had a narrow escape when the end of a substantial rock upon which I had stepped suddenly caved away and went crashing down the mountain.

This gave me an extraordinary sensation. First, there was the immediate, instinctive adjustment to the emergency. I grabbed the gnarled root of an old pine and hung on desperately. In this I had done the right thing without contemplation, in a natural response to the first law of self-preservation. Having pulled myself to safety, I had a sickening stirring in the visceral regions as if, to use a familiar and accurate description, my stomach were "filled with fluttering butterflies." With the incident safely over, and at this comfortable distance, I have named them *Papilio perturbans*, the disturbing swallowtails. I hope the lepidopterists will approve.

Well, I had hung on to that gnarled root, and I had my life. Frankly, I was glad of it. There are still some things which I would like to do.

We sigh because the years, like birds flying, grow faint and small upon the horizon, but in the alchemy of time the present is always the most precious. If we think too deeply of the past, tears mingle with our pride; if we contemplate the future, uncertainty mingles with our hope. But the present is like a magic glass in our minds, focusing both the past and the future into the luminous moment we call now. We must find our happiness in that narrow focus.

Continuing our hike to camp, we noted that the

bark of a large number of evergreen trees had been chewed, in some cases amounting to a complete girdling of the trunk. This is the work of porcupines. These animals are considered pests by the natives, and fair prey to the cowboys' pistols.

Porcupines are vegetarians, living off fruits, grains, bark, and such. Their spines afford protection against other animals, and they live in reasonable security against everything except the cowboys' chance shots. I say "chance shots" because it appears that the average cowboy would rather take a spectacular shot in the general direction and miss, than take more obvious aim and hit, since to him a little bravado is better than a dead porcupine. If, as sometimes happens, that first wild shot actually finds the mark, it will be passed off as an everyday occurrence.

It should not be too hard to find a legitimate use for the porcupine. Although the ranchers do not consider them good food, the Indians are known to eat them. And they seem to fit out here where one always looks before sitting down for fear of sitting upon some unexpected pricker or other.

A rancher named Clyde Malone and his small son rode into camp about six o'clock and stopped to have supper with us, no invitations being necessary in this land of distances. They took their soup and crackers without benefit of bench or table, squatting on their toes, cowboy fashion. Billy has already intimated that our party, which sits at table, is somewhat sissy. When I asked for table and benches with a canvas shelter, I realized from the surprise in his voice that he considered these an affectation. Actually, it is not the comfort we care about so much as the sociability of eating together at table.

The rancher told us more about the coyotes, explaining that there are plenty in the neighborhood, although they are not much in evidence at this season of the year. He pronounced the name "cow-yoats," and demonstrated their bark: one long cry plus a succession of sharp yells, pitched high.

"They are very smart animals," he said. "They know more tricks than Billy."

The coyotes stand as a symbol of our adventure. We do not see them, yet we know they are near. Their tracks sometimes appear in the soft sands of our riverside. Their primitive note suggests the freedom and independence we would like to attain while in the wilderness.

"Clyde kidded Billy," Buttons scribbled, "by telling him that all his equipment at a certain ranch had been chewed by rats and the rest he himself had given to a wandering cowhand. Billy, without a single expression for a give-away, retaliated with a story about Clyde. They seemed to enjoy kidding the pants off each other."

Clyde and his son were as native as the pinyon trees. As they jangled away on their horses they seemed less to disappear than to merge into the landscape. When we could see them no longer, the sound of their spurs still carried, indistinct and musical, through the dusk.

Deep in the night a thunder shower passed on the other side of the mountain. The lightning flashes were vivid, and the rolling echo of the thunder through the valleys and canyons and against the mountainsides was something to remember.

32

The Sixth Chapter

Someone dropped pebbles in our yard,
And one small mountain.

Perhaps the Great Spirit
Was marking His domain,
Or planting pleasant wonders
For His children to explain.

Else why had we discovered
This small and perfect mountain?

F riday, August 22

WEATHER: Fair and cool at 7 A.M. Temperature 55° F.

CONDITION of Party: Good. (I had to argue with Art to persuade him to wash up before breakfast.)

Westerners love their tall stories, and today Wally has swallowed a skyscraper, told by one of the workers from Base Camp: Several years ago the mosquitoes were so bad in this country that one of the natives imported a large number of wasps to combat them, but to his dismay, the plan went wrong, and instead of destroying the mosquitoes, the wasps crossed with them. There resulted a ferocious insect capable of boring at one end like a mosquito, and of stinging like a wasp at the other, rocking back and forth on the poor victim while operating from both ends. This is the "'wasquito."

Actually mosquitoes are not bad here, but flies are plentiful, as they are likely to be in cattle country. We have more than we should because of the dubious camping of our predecessors. At frequent intervals I flail wildly about my tent and slap the sides loudly to drive them out. They leave, but soon return to the shadows of my canvas roof, where they lie in wait to persecute me later by crawling over ears, forehead, nose, or whatever other part may be exposed. I write this as a sug-

34

gestion of gentle torture to be applied to all who, in the future, may leave dirty camp sites.

Billy, disgusted with what he considers an undue adulteration of his morning coffee with hot water and evaporated milk, has recommended duck coffee to Wally and Buttons.

"What do you mean, duck coffee?" asked Buttons.

"Waal, I'll tell you how to git some," said Billy. "You just go down the river about five miles, feed the duck a grain of coffee, and start him off upstream. Then you follow along behind dipping up the water from the rear. That's what I calls duck coffee."

Billy will return to Base Camp this morning to get supplies, and take in and bring out mail. Meanwhile, we will take a lunch to Salt Lake Cave, leaving Bob on guard, and as nursemaid to his poison ivy. During our sojourn here I plan to give each boy at least one "lonely" assignment. It will do him no harm and may provide a needed period of privacy and meditation. It is a poor man who cannot be good company to himself.

Our camp is a compact little community, consisting of six six-by-ten wall tents, a mess fly, the chuck wagon with auxiliary canvas, the corral, garbage pit, latrine, and water supply, all spaced considerably farther apart than they are in this sentence.

The first tent is our headquarters. In it are tables, camp chairs, scientific equipment, records, and small supplies. Its indispensable item, in my estimation, is the portable typewriter with which I type these notes on cheap manila paper. It is actually less a headquarters than an office tent, in the nature of things the busiest spot in camp.

35

The six-by-ten is, of course, a two-man tent, and an excellent size for convenient transportation. Our organization of them is, I believe, ideal. Tops and Irv are close friends, each is seventeen years of age, and both are fond of music and minerals. Naturally, they belong together. Bob and Art are each fifteen, both possessors of a certain integrity of spirit which they will recognize in each other as sterling. They will not shock or jar, but will walk on common ground; therefore they are suitable tentmates. Wally and Buttons are each fourteen years old, and the youngest members of our party. At this age they are likely to argue as to which has done the most, or the least, toward keeping their joint quarters habitable, but they will prefer this to the risk of becoming subservient to an older tentmate who might be tempted to give them orders.

The boys work and travel well together. Wally gets a little more teasing than is good for him, but fortunately he is able to take it. But, observing and hearing these mild intolerances, I sense how little practiced we are in the art of companionship, how needlessly careless and blundering in simple human relationships.

Billy sleeps with the groceries. I do not like this too well, yet in this case it may not make much difference. Most of our foodstuffs are either dry staples or in tin cans, so it seems unlikely that there is any great sanitary risk. Billy, on the other hand, feels that he is protecting our valuable supplies from the "varmints."

We sleep on army-style steel cots with wire springs, but without mattresses, as they are too bulky to transport. Each cot is equipped with a folded canvas tarpaulin upon which we have arranged our sleeping bags. We are comfortable enough, although, as Irv pointed out, "We are not being pampered."

As "Chief" and leader of the group, I have a private tent. This is not selfishness, but seems to me a part of practical leadership. It not only distinguishes the leader in the minds of his men, but it affords him the privacy essential to thoughtful leadership. The wise leader must never give himself away entirely. He must always have something in reserve.

I was put to the test during our travels. We had been riding long hours, and I knew, from experience, that this sustained physical inactivity was not good for the boys. I had to choose between some exercise or a laxative for them.

It happened that there was a fine sunset, and I suggested that they get out of the car in order to enjoy it more. They piled out and walked up a slight embankment to stand beside a fence where they had an excellent view. While waiting, it occurred to me that this was a chance to give them their exercise, so I started the car and drove some distance down the road to wait for them.

I had thought the inference so plain that a spoken order was not necessary. But the boys did not come. Then I realized that they felt that they had been tricked into the hike, and had decided to call my bluff.

I took the quiet opportunity of balancing the expedition's accounts and, after about forty minutes, turned the car around and went back. I hated to spoil the triumph on the boys' faces, but I told them gruffly that when they were ready they would find me waiting at the same place down the road.

They talked it over and came along, but they were very grumpy. I had Tops and Irv ride on the front seat with me and, driving slowly and speaking loudly enough for all to hear, I explained my point of view, and expressed disappointment that they had failed to understand the circumstances.

"I had no reason to trick you," I explained. "Perhaps I was wrong in that I failed to mention specifically that I wanted you to hike to the car. The order could have been put in words simply enough. I do want you to know that it did not occur to me to drive on until you had left the car. You must see that even if I was wrong, as perhaps I was, I could not give in to you and continue to retain my authority. If a leader's authority is successfully challenged in one place, it can be challenged in another."

"But," interrupted Tops, "nobody likes to be humiliated."

"Unfortunately," I replied, "it was your choice. The humiliation was in your own mind. I wouldn't deliberately humiliate anyone." Then I added gently, "Certainly not my best friends. Someday when you are a leader, you may face the same problem, and have to solve it the same way."

"Gosh, Chief, I'm sorry. We didn't understand." Tops would never fail you once he understood. Yet the time may come when he must act on faith.

I had no other occasion for such discipline.

The weather is twice as important to a camper as to anyone else, so a perfect day is recorded with thanksgiving. We ate lunch on the cliff, high above the canyon which lay in a soft purple haze below, the rugged mountains around us extending beyond vision into a sky of billowing white clouds.

Salt Lake Cave yielded some treasure during the day. The number of specimens found was not great, but two of them were thrilling. Both were excavated by Irv, whose chest measurement increased visibly. The first was a bone awl about four inches long, sharp and well polished, and the second was a crescent-shaped pendant of highly polished stone and of superb workmanship. This discovery excited the rest of the party to feverish activity, but they had to be satisfied with potsherds, flint chippings, and doubtful forms.

Digging in caves that have been dry for centuries involves a serious risk of dust poisoning, so we wore handkerchiefs over our noses during the day as protection against the swirling clouds of dust. But these are inadequate masks, and we must improve on them.

We felt the need of a good bath when we returned to camp in the late afternoon, so we stripped, took soap and towels, and went down to the river. The problem was to get clean in a stream running heavy with sediment and itself the color of the brown earth, or of Billy's coffee, according to Art. We have been told that it sometimes runs clear, but we have yet to see it. It was not deep enough for swimming, but the boys found it ideal for mud fighting.

At supper we discussed our findings and their possible significance. Archaeology, defined simply, is the study of ancient man as revealed by what he has left behind him. It is, in practice, a way of digging for buried treasure; treasure which may have no intrinsic value, but which may afford an interpretation of the past. There are two areas of research: the field work, in which the data and materials are collected, and the laboratory work, in which they are studied and interpreted.

You must love the subject in order to enjoy reading the reports of the professionals. As a group, they are remarkable people. But in their reports they are so thorough that a coroner, following their technique in an autopsy, would have to count every hair on a dead man's chest, and list and catalogue each separately as "supporting data."

Archaeologists are the most underpaid and, at the same time, the most overprivileged men I know. They do not earn enough to keep the shine out of the seat of their trousers, but they find adventure around every corner. Their writings may be dull, but they are peerless conversationalists, with enough knowledge of man and his history not to take themselves too seriously. Most of them are pure scientists who would starve to death if it were not for a few wise universities, museums, and millionaires. They are almost too good to be true, and their writings too true to be good.

A huge boulder rests in the center of our camp, massive and imperturbable, like a little mountain in our yard. The trails wind either side of it, and our lives over and around it as we pass. Clothes and sleeping bags are aired on it, and laundry is sometimes left to dry. Seated on this boulder, one surveys the camp. It is a meeting place, and from it we challenge the stars with our talk. Beside it we have built our council fire, burning the fragrant canyon timbers more for incense than for warmth.

It was Tops who marshaled the fellows and, with their

help, constructed the fine stone fireplace on the west side of the boulder.

It is man's nature to love a fire. It is warmth to his body and balm to his spirit. Seated, thinking, beside a fire, he brings the heritage of the race into focus, and rests his thoughts on the warm bosom of time after the fashion of his fathers. Men in every age have gone forth from their campfires to do valiant and thoughtful deeds. Those who become too civilized to enjoy a fire have lost, rather than gained, in culture.

Our first-aid kit is getting daily use, usually for minor cuts and scratches. Bob is the prize patient tonight, having both poison ivy and a ripening boil. Tops, having had a tetanus antitoxin last week, will be due for a reaction in a few days, and all because he tried to jump a barbed-wire fence. Choosing a moment when all eyes were upon him, he attempted to hurdle the fence while loaded down with mineral specimens. No failure could have been staged more dramatically and the look of hurt surprise in his eyes was such that I could not be harsh with him, although I was genuinely exasperated. I had warned that barbed-wire injuries in cattle country would require prompt antitetanus treatment, and now Tops had thirty inches of scratches to be treated. In spite of the unmerciful ribbing given him by the other members of the party, he made no effort to defend himself. The star of the Hopkins Grammar School track team had fallen, and he knew it.

Billy is back from Base with mail, and off again "to snag in a load of wood." He chooses seasoned roots and the pieces which require the least cutting, on the theory that it is foolish for a man to do work which nature may already have done for him.

Clyde Malone, the rancher who was here last night, advanced an interesting theory to explain the abundance of wild sunflowers. He says they were not common prior to the dust storms in the plains states a few years back, and he believes the seeds were blown in with the clouds of dust from the dust bowl.

Malone himself won the affection of our gang with his genial boisterousness. Once, in the middle of the night, he passed through camp on his way home from rodeo, paying his respects with a wild, loud yell. We were not offended. His personality seems a part of this flamboyant and uninhibited land.

At dusk Venus twinkled in the triangle of the two mountains which watch over us from the southwest, so brilliant above the darkly silhouetted peaks that it, alone, seemed star enough for any sky.

"The last thing I heard," wrote Buttons in his diary, "was Tops and Irv laughing in their tent near by and I was glad that we could be carefree so far away from home."

The Seventh Chapter

On the trail he found a blue jay's feather
Which he wears skyward in his hat
To please himself, and never mind the weather.
He is a man; he is too big for that.

Saturday, August 23

WEATHER: Fair. Temperature at 7 A.M. 61° F.

CONDITION of Party: Steady.

Aquila, the eagle! I saw him high among the crags at dawn. Then, majestically, he soared into the canyon and over the mountain.

In his limitless world of air the great bird seemed more than ever a symbol of liberty, not glittering and fixed as on our silver coins, but vivid and alive in his mastery of the sky.

I had known, as woodsmen do, that the day confers its best gifts upon those who rise with the dawn. To birds and animals this is instinctive. They do not remain in their leafy hiding places, or their dark burrows, after the first light. They meet each morning as though it were the first, for in the wilderness the day always begins in innocence.

This morning, for the first time, we begin drinking the water from our well without treating it. After finding the dead muskrat in it the day we arrived, we pumped it as nearly dry as we could, and then bailed until our pail had lost its handle and we our patience. It was a task requiring several hours of hard work and some ingenuity. We used every chlorine tablet we had, dumping them into the well after dissolving them, and, in addition, treating the individual pails of drinking water with iodine in the ratio of one drop to a quart,

44

allowed to stand twenty minutes before drinking.

"It made your mouth seem tight and wrinkled," said Bob.

At three-forty-five this afternoon we decided to abandon Salt Lake Cave. We had gone down to sterile soil in more than two-thirds of the cave, and made test digs in the remainder. I doubt if we left much. Today's findings included more chips, additional sherds, another bone awl, and some casual specimens of woods and grasses.

It is doubtful if, at this stage, I should attempt an extended interpretation of the materials found in Salt Lake Cave. This is a task which should wait, anyway, until after the laboratory work has been done. The location of the cave, high in the cliffs, probably discouraged any Indians from living there for a long period.

Water, in dry weather, must have been a serious problem. During the rainy season the small streams on the slope above may have provided an adequate supply of water, but they are dry now, and a resident in the cave would have to bring water up from the river below. We brought canteens full to brimming and, in addition, a three-gallon milk can, counting the labor less than the hardship of doing without. Water is life, and where there is little water, there can be little life. This would be our fundamental deduction about Salt Lake Cave.

The cave provides good shelter from the elements and, as such, was probably a convenient stopping place. Hunters would have found it accessible both from the high lands above and the canyon floor below. No doubt it was used, too, as temporary quarters for more than one Indian family; but I do not believe that any brave

45

would have selected it as a permanent place in which to hang his G string.

Since Thursday we have been intrigued by a plateau, or mesa, about one-quarter of the way up the mountain on the opposite side of the canyon from Salt Lake Cave. This comparatively level and verdant area of several acres looks like a favorable spot for Indian agriculture, so we decided to explore it this afternoon. We found a number of flint chips and the upper half of what had once been a very fine quartz arrowhead.

In the cliff beneath the mesa is another cave, but it has seen much use by cowboys and others, and has obviously been subjected to promiscuous digging. Our immediate problem is to decide what to do tomorrow; whether to return to this cave and dig, explore the mesa further, or look into a couple of shelters near our camp which invite closer inspection. The heavy rains of this season have caused such rank growth in the flats and open spaces that the determination of ancient camp sites, other than cliff dwellings, is especially difficult.

Art is our cartographer. He took careful measurements in Salt Lake Cave and is now making a preliminary drawing on graph paper showing the location of each of the important artifacts discovered. Later he will make a permanent copy with India ink. Looking over his shoulder and observing the care he is taking, I appreciate that a good job is in the making.

Meanwhile, Wally has brought his first batch of films out of the developer with a perfect score! This is an undeniable triumph for him, and he is celebrating by singing the juke-box melody of 1941, "You Are My

Sunshine." His rendition is not the nostalgic recorded variety. It sparkles with enthusiasm.

Earlier in the day Wally had wept with frustration. His photography requires sterile water and, with great pains, he had brought some to a boil only to have a gust of wind sprinkle soot and ashes over it.

"Ouch! My water is ruined!" he cried, and Billy, taking him literally, replied, "Then you won't be needin' it," and dropped in his dirty socks.

Wally didn't say a word in reply but he sat disconsolately on a log, with set jaw and clenched fists, as the noiseless tears rolled down his cheeks.

We have seen many deer tracks since we came in on location and today we saw our first deer, a fine doe which climbed the hill above us as we searched the mesa. A favorite joke with the boys at Philmont is to yell "Deer!", wait for you to look up, and then add, "tracks."

There are wild-cat tracks, too, and on the way back to camp this afternoon Tops and Wally saw four wild turkeys. Other animals which are indigenous to the ranch, but which we have not seen, include elk, mountain lions, antelope, beaver, prairie dogs, and a decimated herd of buffalo. Fortunately all are protected, as hunting is not permitted within the reservation.

We have not made face-to-face acquaintance with the pack rats, which is probably no great loss. They have left their droppings by the ton in the cliffs and crevices of the canyons. One of the boys remarked that we do everything except inhale these remains, as they have enough weight to keep them from flying around in the dust.

47

"Now I know," he added, brushing them off his overalls, "why they call these *dung*arees."

The pack rat, according to Billy, is about ten inches long with a tail of equal length which is slightly bushy at the tip. The color, he adds, is a dirty, yellowish brown. Otherwise the creature is completely ratlike. I hope the Indians found some use for him. We have not.

Smaller mice chew our things at night, their gnawings sounding loud in the nocturnal quiet. The slightest movement, and they flash away into the darkness, never remaining long enough to be caught in the beam of our flashlights but they return when we have been still a while.

The rock wren deserves a more favorable notice. It is very common and comparatively tame, a delight to watch and to hear. While at Base one kept us company as we explored the cliffs above the lodge. Since, the song of these wrens has been a part of every morning and every dusk, and much of the time in between.

The sound reminds me of the high giggle schoolgirls make when amused at something they think a bit naughty. The rock wren, leading so songlike an existence, in a place of such charm, should be one of the happiest of birds. The nest is usually built in a cleft among the rocks, and is constructed of twigs, hair, mosses, wool, or grass, with a paving in front made of small pebbles, pieces of glass, or rock.

I have been pleased with Buttons. Last night he went to bed tired and supperless, and I thought that he might have a touch of homesickness. With his fourteen tender years separated by over two thousand miles from a gra-

48

cious home, his weariness may have led his thoughts homeward. He said he was only sleepy, supper being late, and that may have been all. Today he is completely recovered, and master of himself. Cheerful and industrious, willing and co-operative, he has earned his spurs as an expedition member. On the way back from the dig, he wore, jauntily, a bright blue feather in his hat.

The sunset was a study in contrasting reds, blues, and golds, dominating a pattern indescribably delicate above the dark mountain. Neither gaudy nor splashy, it was toned gently for remembrance on some cold, gray, Eastern day. Now we begin to understand the magic of the mountains. There is the spacious sweep of vision, the rarefied air, the vigorous climbing, and the ever present touch of danger in the contest between man and mountain, and always some slight question as to which shall be master.

"Lucky for us," says Tops, "the mountain has no brains."

The Eighth Chapter

COWBOY SONG: To be sung to the tune
of "My Bonnie Lies over the Ocean."

Oh, there will be only one cowboy,
  When we dream of our ranch in the West
For Billy will ride on before us,
  Singing the songs we love best.

CHORUS:

Ride on, ride on,
  Ride on to Philmont,
Ride on, ride on.
Ride on, ride on,
  Ride on to Philmont, ride on.

The wide world may be our dominion,
  And cowboys by dozens display,
But if you should ask our opinion,
  We would ride beside Billy each way.

NOTE: Other scouts are granted permission to
substitute the name of their favorite cowboy.

Sunday, August 24

WEATHER: Fair. Temperature at 7 A.M. 56° F.
Much warmer during the day.

CONDITION of Party: More, or less, devout.

My tent is pitched within a few feet of the river which,
like the stream in "Kubla Khan," runs unceasingly and
musically on. Awakening deep in the night and hearing
its flow, I am reminded of Cornell and Ithaca, the myriad
waterfalls of the Finger Lakes.

Since it is Sunday we decided to modify our program
to semiholiday. We shall breakfast late this morning,
work until a late lunch, and leave the remainder of the
day for optional activities.

Art, conscientious to a degree, debated the possibility
of hiking over the rugged trails to attend Mass, but the
uncertainties on the other end were too discouraging.
The nearest Mass may be in Cimarron, or in Raton, for
all we know. Cimarron is small, in a country more given
to taverns than to chapels.

So Art has retired to a quiet place with his prayer
book. As the traveler turns to Polaris, he seeks the eternal and the true. Yet, the best has never been farther
away than his own good and stalwart heart.

Every man carries a shrine within himself, a well of
deep emotion, full of happiness and tears. It has its dark
mysteries, of which the deepest is his inability ever to explain himself. In the end, he is the child who, seeking

52

beyond the veil of God's work, inquires: "Yes, but *who* made God?" And he can never escape; for every cup of experience from that well is sweet or bitter with wonder, and he may not cease to puzzle over the things which he shall never know; there remaining enough mystery in one leaf to dust him with the ashes of despair.

I hinted some of these thoughts to Billy, who nodded understandingly and then remarked, "But you won't feel that way after you have had your cup of coffee." Needless to say, my serious thoughts departed with my laughter.

The best story today is one which Billy told about our breakfast milk. Wally and Buttons believe it, to the amusement of their wiser comrades. As the first boy reached for the milk, Billy slapped him on the wrist.

"Now, you be careful how much of that milk you take," he said. "That's all there is."

"But why?" asked Buttons. "I thought we had plenty."

"Waal," says Billy, "that's deer's milk."

Then he spun a more or less plausible yarn about having roped a doe back in the corral this morning. His description of the trouble he had holding off the hungry fawn was classic.

"... and I finally had to kick the poor little critter," he ended sadly.

Impressed, Wally and Buttons tasted the milk experimentally. They agreed that it was not much different from our regular supply, a mixture of half-and-half tinned evaporated milk and water, but that the deer's milk was a bit richer. They probably won't know the truth until they read this. They have not yet learned to be suspicious of that twinkle in Billy's eye.

During the morning we explored a series of small near-by caves. Irv headed a party consisting of himself, Tops, and Bob, checking on the shelters in the canyon to our north. I crossed the river with the others to investigate the small canyon to our west.

Test digs made by both parties were negative, so the day has been practically fruitless, archaeologically. We uncovered a few chips in the crevices behind the petroglyphs west of camp, and these tempt us to explore that locality further.

Returning to camp just before one o'clock we found visitors. Miss Dawson, the daughter of the director, Mr. Smith (my failure to remember his first name makes him practically anonymous), and Bob Bereton of the Base Trading Post. They wanted moving pictures of digging and climbing, so we donned shirts and neckerchiefs in order to oblige. The pictures, if good, are scheduled to appear in a general movie of Philmont.

Irv has an incorrigible case of boulderitis, which may be defined as a mania for tumbling mountains into valleys. No loose stone or boulder is safe if he is near, but is sent hurtling and crashing down the mountainside, to the great alarm of the gophers and small animals for half a mile around. Irv, standing triumphantly on the brink, utters delighted exclamations, and looks for another part of the mountain to tear away. Now Bob has been taken with the same infection.

It is midafternoon and the party is relaxing according to individual preferences. Irv is washing clothes, Tops reading *Famous English and Irish Detective and Mystery*

54

Stories, Wally singing over his photography, and the rest writing letters, except Billy, who has disappeared into the recesses of his tent for a siesta. It is an intense day, ameliorated by an occasional pleasant breeze and periodic cloud banks, but when the sun is out, as Billy says, "it really bears down on you."

The most touching scene of the day was Billy seated near the two-strand wire fence which he has constructed to keep the horses, Dan and Prince, within bounds. He was mending his blankets (which seemed already pathetically past being worth the trouble) and talking to his horses. "Hyar there, no fudgin'," he said in a tone more of pride than admonition, as the horses stretched their necks over the fence in an effort to graze as near to him as possible. I have sometimes wondered about the lap-poodle lovers, but there is sense in the cowboy's feeling for his horse. It is, I believe, the deepest affection any man bears for an animal.

Most animal pets are patronized, but the cowboy's horse is not. He is recognized as the faithful friend and companion of the trails. If there have been adventures, he has shared them; if there have been hardships, he has known them, too. Plodding the long range in silence and in patience, he has become one with his rider, helping to keep his sentiment alive and to fix his calm philosophy. For the cowboy has time to think and with his thoughts to ride, without care, into the future.

Tops pontificated this afternoon that the two greatest short-story writers that ever lived were Poe and De Maupassant. I debated the point briefly, pointing out that Poe was habitually morose and that De Maupassant rarely thought above the belt, but Tops, according to his custom, will not admit that he is wrong. That is, not before day after tomorrow.

Billy, speaking with solemn weather wisdom, informs us that our moon will not hold water, and consequently we shall have fine weather. I hope the law of averages is on his side and that the right of every man to have one prophecy in ten come true will be fulfilled in him. After he had finished the dishes, we sat for an hour around the chuck fire singing songs and listening to his reminiscences of cattle doings. Talk of roping, branding, driving, feeding, and the general orneriness of the breed gave us some of the real flavor of the range.

Billy, squatting on his toes, rolling his own cigarettes, and grinning out from beneath his straw hat, was the personification of cowboy. It was his hour; and if he relished the attention and respect accorded by the boys, it was a small vanity, the honor not less than his due.

"Billy is just like a story-book cowboy," Buttons noted, "and we hold him in the light of a genius."

Art accounted for the day in his usual brief paragraph:

"Sunday, but no chance to go to Mass. Wasted good time on a bum cave. Miss Dawson and two men-in-waiting came to dinner. Spruced up and had pictures taken for something. Had deer milk for breakfast, canned, ha! ha! Everybody sleepy and went to bed after a bull, or cow, session around the fire."

At dusk Venus reappeared at the triangle of the mountains and, as though the day of miracles had not passed, a thin crescent moon beneath it.

Through the open doorway of my tent, while lying on my cot, I saw Corona Borealis, then Aquila, then Delphinus dip westward and gradually disappear behind the

56

mountain. I shall remember this night and its stars. Restless, I thought I could see beyond our dark mountain to the stark and violent world, already flaming with war. And as I thought of my sleeping young companions, and the uncertainties of their tomorrows, I could not rest, but tucked the swinging constellations behind the mountains, one by one, through the long night.

The Ninth Chapter

Where are the hunters now, the tall braves of the roving bands?
Do they have sharp arrows that will wing the stars in spirit lands?
Are they hunting Leo, Orion, or Scorpio, past the meridian?
Have they the turquoise still, the flashing eagle feathers, and obsidian?

Monday, August 25

My son, Forrest Agassiz, is eight years old today. To think of him is to enjoy the feeling one has in listening to a pastoral symphony; one, I should add, like Beethoven's, which has occasional outbursts of thunder and lightning.

The chief adventure of the morning went to Bob, who was struck at by a rattlesnake, chopped it in two with the shovel he was carrying, and excitedly brought the rear end, including ten rattles, for inspection. The way we dress takes such eventualities into consideration. We normally wear high leather shoes and long dungarees, or levis. We also have a special suction kit for the treatment of snake bite which every member of the party knows how to use.

The last time I was in Freeport, Maine, I stopped at Bean's to purchase a few dry flies for trout fishing, but fell victim, as I usually do, to other temptations. The clerk sold me a pair of forest-green shooting pants with a convenient zipper fly. An elderly down-east Yankee had preceded me, but he refused to buy the zippered garment because, he said, "I ain't goin' to be pinched in the same place twice."

Actually the short-waisted levis such as cowboys wear

60

are best for this country, although, in my opinion, they might be improved a bit by that zipper.

Bob could not describe the sound of the snake very well. "It just rattled," he said. Bret Harte described it as "a sound of dry leaves that stir in the valley." Cabeca de Vaca's description, given perhaps four hundred years earlier, was even better. He called it a "fearful serpent with castanets in its tail."

Here is Bob's story of his encounter with the snake:

"We set out in high hopes of excitement and I met five feet of it. On this one day I had left my boots because they irritated my poison ivy. Consequently I had to take off my sneakers to wade the river. This delay put me behind my companions who had gone on ahead. I was carrying a shovel, a geologist's pick, and other impedimenta.

"Down the trail I sauntered when, suddenly, I saw a strange gray-green coil at my feet. It proved to be very resilient, for as I jumped over it, it made a lightning stab at one of my sneakers. My stars were lucky and it missed.

"I stopped a moment to make sure what it was, for its unexpected appearance had left me quite dazed. There he was, a big rattler, sliding off into the tall grass! I took a quick swipe at him with the shovel for I didn't intend to have the affair unavenged. I'll bet he was surprised because I cut off about a foot of his end. I impaled this on the pick and tore off down the trail with my gory trophy.

"I did not look into the brush for the rest of the snake, because I had had enough. Neither could I describe how

I felt because a poor description would have belittled my reeling emotions."

Naturally, I did not blame Bob for killing the snake, though I thought to myself that it need not have been killed. It might, happily, have escaped to a harmless old age, for at ten years it was already reasonably venerable in snake ways. The things of nature do not need to justify themselves to man.

According to Liberty Hyde Bailey, things were not made for man alone. There was logic, he says, in the farmer's retort to the good man who told him that roses were made to make men happy. "No, they weren't," said the farmer, "or they wouldn't a had prickers." A teacher once asked Bailey what snakes are good for and he replied, "They are good to be snakes." Yet people are so afraid of them that even the harmless ones suffer.

Bob's adventure reminded me of another story. A native was struck in his wooden leg by a rattler. The leg began to swell so that he couldn't put on or take off his pants and, in shaving it down to size, he accumulated enough kindling for the winter.

During the morning we investigated the cave beneath the mesa. We threw out the supply of old railroad ties in order to dig our test trenches, a deed for which we shall probably be cussed some cool day this fall if the cowboys stop to build a fire.

The dig itself was nothing to brag about. The cave had been exhaustively tunneled by relic seekers, and the four trenches which we dug yielded little in the way of artifacts: an obsidian chip, a bone tool, and two small sherds similar to the ones found in Salt Lake Cave.

We climbed the cliffs to the mesa to eat our lunch,

after which we spent some time searching its surface. In one small area we picked up eleven arrowheads, practically all of them imperfect because of breakage. The typical arrowheads of this area are small and crude, normally less than an inch long, and usually of poor flint, although sometimes of quartz or obsidian. Irv found the largest number, although Buttons picked up a good quartz specimen. The heat was severe and at about four o'clock we decided to return to camp for a bath and rest.

Tops and Art, who had remained to work near camp, reported some success in the cave adjacent to the Indian Writings. They had uncovered a number of flint chips, a good projectile point, and a fine flint scraper. We have decided to concentrate upon this and another near-by cave tomorrow.

A message from Rodney Cobb of the University of Oklahoma brought the welcome news that he plans to spend the Labor Day week end with us, so we dispatched Billy to Base Camp via horseback with letters of arrangement. We had stopped in Norman, where the university is located, on the way out in order to visit the Anthropological Laboratory and in the expectation that Cobb would join our expedition. We were keenly disappointed when we found that he could not. But we had been magnificently entertained.

An enormous red ant makes its home in this country. It lives in immense colonies under a granulated mound of earth from one to two feet in height, and at the center of a circular area which I found, by pacing, to average twelve to eighteen feet in diameter. This entire area remains barren in spite of the rank growth which surrounds it on all sides. I cut into one heap and found the area of occupation within the mound itself. The ants reacted violently to my ruthlessness and the entire heap was soon covered with agitated members of the colony. One of the boys who was bitten by them reported that "They are no fun."

I asked Billy the name of these ants and he replied, "piss ants." They are so called because it is reputed that they will, after biting, void a highly acid urine into the wound which causes it to smart painfully.

We came across some scouts from Wichita on their way up the mountain, and since they were interested in Salt Lake Cave, we asked if they would save us another trip up by bringing down a fine log specimen which we had taken for tree-ring checking. They obligingly threw it four-fifths of the way down, and we had to search the other fifth in order to find it, reflecting meanwhile that it is sometimes possible to be accommodating without being gracious.

The log specimen might be of great value to us in determining the date when Salt Lake Cave was occupied. This is because of the remarkable research of Dr. A. E. Douglas of the University of Arizona, which has resulted in an accurate chronology of the Southwest.

It is elementary with the botanist that the width of the annual growth rings in trees varies with the amount of moisture they receive. A wet year will be reflected in a wide growth ring, and a drought year in a narrow one. Dr. Douglas assumed, correctly, that the growth patterns of contemporary trees in a specific area would be identical, while differing from those of trees in any other period. Starting from this point Dr. Douglas, who was seeking to correlate the incidence of sun spots with the earth's climate, made a striking and unexpected contribution to archaeology. He hit upon the brilliant idea of matching the growth rings of living trees of known age with those of more ancient timbers. Following this procedure it was possible to work out a tree-ring calendar in the Southwest which dates back to 11 A.D., and it may go further!

The process is not as simple as it sounds, as there are many complications, but the fact remains that if we are fortunate enough to get a few good tree-ring specimens, we shall be able to date our excavations here to the exact year. The name of this new science is dendrochronology.

I found that Bob had mixed mud and sky in a brilliant paragraph:

"The sky we had with our lunch was the most beautiful I had ever seen. The zenith was a deep azure, a color no sapphire could rival. This incomparable blue faded to the horizon where, because of the distance, it looked like a weak water color. When we got home, hot and weary, the river welcomed us with its elixir of life, and Irv and I had a glorious mud fight."

When they came up from the creek after the mud fight they had splattered and daubed each other beyond recognition. After the hilarious part was over neither wanted to be the first to cry, "Hold, enough!"

I warned the fellows before we left New Haven that we would be miles away from chocolate sodas, funnies, movies, radios, and girls, a prediction which has been literally true. I deposited our funds with Mr. Dawson at Base Camp, bringing only a small amount with me, for which I have had absolutely no demand. We have been living on a formula which does not require the daily exchange of money, and it is good.

Unwritten in this journal, but felt deeply, is a certain sense of escape from worry and responsibility; no word of war, no telephone, radio, or newspaper; just wideness and wildness, crag upon crag, sky of clouds and sky of stars, rugged, clean, and free.

There is a snap in the air tonight with intimations of frosty mornings to come. There has been no rain for three days, and the river begins to appear noticeably clearer. Irv believes the glittering little specks in the river sand may actually be silver. He does not think they are mica.

Buttons, remembering his training at Peabody, thought he had discovered something unusual in the potsherds he was working with this afternoon, in that they appeared to be tempered with both sand and shell, whereas his instructor at Peabody had stated that it was normally one or the other, rarely both. Then the silver specks in our little river gave the clue to the fact: Temper from these sands will give the shell-like specks characteristic of shell-tempered pottery.

It must be recorded as a minor miracle that Art did not mention baseball today. For a career he thinks he will choose between professional baseball and the diplomatic service. Meanwhile, he has gone a long way when even the New York Yankees, his favorite team, has faded out, for the time, in favor of cave plottings and archaeological palaver.

"It's great talking to Art," said Tops. "For all of his fifteen years he acts much older, and can talk on serious subjects with facility. I like and admire him very much."

Tops, himself, as I have remarked before, has reached the senile age of seventeen.

Billy brought some surgical gauze back from Base, which Bob and I made into masks for tomorrow's adventures in the caves. These will be a tremendous improvement over the handkerchiefs we have been using.

The boys have been going down to the river to wash clothes from time to time and, this afternoon, I had to take my turn. This is sanitary air, full of health and zest. This afternoon the wind was brisk, and hiking face into it, one seemed to carry a little hurricane in each ear. The sun and wind dry small things in just twenty minutes.

Night! Rest from the bright sun in the shadowy peace of the stars. We will not be strangers to this land again. One boy is singing, and there is in his voice more than the melody or the words. There is serenity and joy.

> "How often at night, when the heavens are bright,
> With the light of the glittering stars...
> Have I stood there amazed, and asked as I gazed,
> If their glory exceeds that of ours."

He is humming it now. Philmont is an inspired place, of the normal earth a second cousin, twice removed, and yet bringing the corners of the nation together as the accents of Texas and Oklahoma meet those of New England, Pennsylvania, and the Northwest. One escapes from the world, and yet meets it again in the hiking scouts who hail from over the hills and far away.

I am certain that Waite Phillips, who gave this site to scouting, sensed the inspiring quality of his gift, because he knows and loves this Western land. He deserves well of his native country, for he has served it well. Having been here, I shall never question the desirability of having as many boys come to Philmont as can, and from whatever distances.

All is quiet in camp; my boys asleep. I feel that they belong to me for these few weeks even more than they do to their parents. They are like sons and brothers, not quite perfect, but worthy and loyal above their small faults: supercilious Tops, who likes to complain, but doesn't very much; conscientious Irv, who, because he has interests of his own, would sometimes like to shirk, but won't; calm and steady Bob, who does his part without questioning, and doesn't get excited short of an encounter with a rattlesnake; thoughtful and loyal Art, who never fails to do his best; good-natured Wally, who is lazy in some things, but diligent in his photography; and fun-loving Buttons, with his marvelous raised eyebrow and muffled giggle, who is a tonic of quiet gaiety for us all. Let the coyotes howl and the pack rats gnaw my choicest leather; these are my companions, and with them I am well content.

The Tenth Chapter

A lad stood on the shores
of the Mississippi,
And a yearning in his spirit stirred,
in vain,
To ride upon its crest until
he reached the sea.
It was a vast futility—
his first remembered pain—
He could not leave it on that shore.
It always came again.

Tuesday, August 26

WEATHER: Fair. Temperature at 7 A.M. 61° F.

CONDITION of Party: Slightly wavering.

Since our first night on the prairie, en route to Philmont, we have had tick inspections at regular intervals to avoid the possibility of Rocky Mountain spotted fever. Stripped to their birthday clothes, the boys look each other over carefully for the dangerous insect.

"You can't be modest at the risk of harboring one of those babies," says Irv.

"But what gets me," commented Art, "is that they can't tell us from a cow."

No ticks had been discovered until this morning, when I found one crawling on my pillow. He was beautifully flat and thin, apparently not having had an opportunity to attach himself; this to my great relief. Probably it would have made no difference, as there is no record of infected ticks in this vicinity. But we have no desire to furnish the first case history.

We spent the morning working in three adjacent caves which we unimaginatively named Indian Writing Caves A, B, and C. A yielded a few flint chippings, and C a number of chips and a few potsherds. B stands for barren.

A party of Pennsylvania scouts, hot but cheerful, came over the mountain to see the petroglyphs. They arrived while we were eating lunch and remained politely aloof while waiting for the rest of their party, twenty-two in all. The savory odors from our table made some of them fidgety, but they would not eat until their entire party had arrived. After lunch one of them interpreted the Indian Writings for us:

"Having a swell time. Wish you were here."

Later they watched us excavate for a while, asking questions and giving our party an unusual opportunity to act important. But our luck was poor, and we did not turn up anything exciting while they were around.

"However," Buttons reported, "I showed them the artifacts from Salt Lake Cave and was very much satisfied with their looks of awe."

Their interpretation of the petroglyphs, given so facetiously, was probably not far from the truth. Our deduction is that they were carved by Plains Indians who were using the canyon as a passage in their travels. This would be after the reintroduction of horses into America by the Spaniards, as the petroglyphic drawings include actual portrayals of horses. This also means that the writings could not be contemporaneous with our black and white sherds, which are unquestionably early Pueblo. Therefore we are dealing with two primitive cultures which were probably separated from each other by several hundred years.

The horse may have had its origin in America. Early records reveal him as a small animal, hardly more than a foot high, and about the size of a fox. He had four toes and a rudimentary fifth, instead of one hoof as he does now. There was a long period of evolution in between. Luckily he was a venturesome animal and, in his travels, crossed the land bridge at Bering Strait into other continents, where he spread and flourished. For, by the end of the glacial period, for reasons which we do not know, the horse had become extinct in America. When he was reintroduced by the early Spaniards, the horse was utterly unknown to the inhabitants. They had no myth or legend to suggest this as his former home, he had been gone so long. Not since Folsom man, approximately ten thousand years ago, has there been evidence of his association with man in the new world.

Irv has been a little impatient with Wally for his loafing, but Wally's inertia is, I believe, purely physiological, part of the strain of growing up. Mentally he is alert as a hawk and, while working with his pictures, he sings happy, though wordless, melodies.

I can remember a time when the hardest work I wanted to do was to go swimming and when my favorite recreation was to daydream. I lived on a lake and wanted, most of all, to find the most beautiful pearl in the world. I may never know Wally's dreams, but I am sure they are fine ones. Perhaps, some day, he will find the beautiful pearl. As a lad I thought of it as a jewel to be taken from a mussel shell on the shores of my southern lake. It is different now, and harder to find. Its name is Truth.

This has been a day of hard labor without any results to speak of. To me it is of no particular consequence, but to my young explorers it is discouraging. Tops has set his heart upon finding turquoise, which is known to have been the special treasure of the Indians.

During the day Tops and Art finished Cave A, and Bob and Irv found little in Cave C. In Cave B we unearthed the cross-sections of two fire pits, one about five inches below the surface, and the other about seven inches deeper. I had Wally photograph these, as there is an interesting time interval to consider. The earlier of these fires may have been built by the residents of the cliffs, say a thousand years ago, and the latter may be what remains of a campfire built by the Plains Indians, traveling through on horseback, hundreds of years later.

The party took a lively interest in the restoration of the pot from Salt Lake Cave, upon which Art and Buttons made considerable progress during the day. Its contours are now well established although several important sherds are missing. It is a good specimen and is, I believe, a typical early Pueblo utility vessel. It is about twelve inches tall, flares from the neck to about eight inches in diameter at the middle, and then narrows to a base of about four or five inches. It has two opposite handle nodules just below the rim, and is flaked with the soot of ancient fires.

Art and Buttons took an absorbing interest in mixing plaster of Paris with various pigments in an effort to match the Salt Lake vessel, trying for a formula which would retain sufficient color without the loss of basic strength.

The natural desire of a boy to experiment is one of the most hopeful indications of the progress of the race. As long as we have youngsters who want to know what makes the wheels go around, we shall continue to advance.

Wandering along the shores of Lake Cayuga, years ago, I found a boy on his hands and knees lapping up water with his tongue.

"What on earth are you doing?" I asked.

"Oh, just trying to find out how a dog drinks water,"

he replied. "It must be by suction as I can't get much this way, but of course a dog has a longer tongue."

I know that was a good experiment, because I got down on my hands and knees and tried it with him.

Billy gave us a fine supper which included meat, potatoes, corn, sour-dough biscuits, jam, tea, and stewed raisins. His sour-dough biscuits, which we are now having twice a day, are Rembrandts of cooking, masterpieces of the Dutch oven. Bob watched him make them and recorded it as follows:

"It was amusing to watch Billy mix his sour-dough biscuits. He kept the mix in a large crock. Whenever he took any out, he mixed a little more in. In a bowl he would put a few handfuls of flour, then a pinch of salt, a bit of baking powder, a shake of sugar, and a can or so of milk. He never actually measured it out in a cup. He knew just the right amount to put in. Then he would stir this concoction with his 'boot.' His boot is his hand! Where on earth he got this name for it I don't know. But I do know that he is famous in all this country for his sour-dough biscuits."

Billy is the first more or less intimate acquaintance which the boys have ever had with "a real cowboy" and they are delighted with him. They also have a natural curiosity concerning his welfare, as is revealed in Tops's diary of this date:

"Irv and I had a long talk with Billy about cowpunching, wages, and the international situation. Billy is a little dissatisfied with the wage scale around here, and I hardly blame him. Billy is a great fellow and worth a lot more than he is getting. He says some of the cow punchers are paid a measly twenty-five dollars a month.

Billy is getting about forty-five. This is tough, and I hope he finds something better. I think he has ability as well as good brains, a sense of pleasing conversation, and a likeable personality.

"I found out from him that he is married, a thing that I have suspected. He has a kid that is ready for school. He can only see them every so often because of his work. Sometimes he is away from them for a month at a time. But that is the life of a cowboy."

The boys are sociable as a flock of crows, and table talk, on the whole, is pleasant and uninhibited. Only rarely does one of them get out of bounds. I try not to bar any subject, but at meals a degree of convention seems desirable. It is our custom to offer silent grace before eating. We carry our own packs, and each his own weight of thanks.

The boys are sometimes amusingly vulgar, but they are never obscene. I am glad they are free from restraint and inhibition, the two qualities which serve as armor against those whom we do not fully trust.

Billy has ceremoniously hung out the bacon for the night, explaining that he needs to give it an airing. He doesn't say why. Perhaps he feels it may keep better if it absorbs some of the night chill before he packs it away in the morning.

Following supper we used our fireplace in front of the great rock again. Howls, groans, and clammy fingers accompanied my ghost story. These gave rise to an incipient plot to scare Wally but, getting wind of it, I chased the boys to bed.

It is bedtime, and our fire is burning low. Tops and Irv are talking quietly with Billy, and the younger boys

75

are asleep. We haven't seen a newspaper or heard the radio so we do not know and, for the moment, we do not care what the news is. We have taken a little time out, and do not wish to spoil it with the quinine of reality.

Our little river runs clearer every day, and so it has been with us. Gradually we have forgotten our ordinary cares, as our days have grown brighter and clearer. We are living in an oasis. Before long we must return to school and desk. When we do we hope to have a new readiness for life, having in our hearts the wealth of the mountains and in our minds the memory of our travels together.

Here the small cares of everyday are healed, and the graver ones are blurred so that one realizes them indistinctly as something one should remember, but can almost forget. If one could, in the middle of life, find such a retreat in which to rest from the commonplace for a year, in something more commonplace and simple than he has ever known, then he might return, as in a renaissance, to the worldly tasks which give him his illusion of greatness.

The good life is to be wiser tomorrow than today. We should not care whether anyone else senses it, as long as we can feel it within ourselves. Failure to broaden one's horizons is, ultimately, to be restricted to the narrow ranges of the past. We should not be content to wander aimlessly among the foothills of experience. We should climb the mountains if we can.

The Eleventh Chapter

If we can trust tomorrow,
I think that we will find
The world is just as wide
As music in the mind.

There is no fatal sorrow
In the anguish that we feel;
There is no pain or bitterness
Which beauty cannot heal.

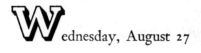

Wednesday, August 27

WEATHER: Cloudy at 6:30 A.M. Fair since, with immense billowing white clouds.

CONDITION of Party: Fair, to much better.

Morale, which has been exceptionally high, took a nose dive yeterday afternoon. Work was a bit desultory then, and has continued so this morning. We have labored hard in barren ground and my youthful party has been put to a severe test, since they have lacked the incentives of discovery. Tops has been as petulant as an assistant vice-president with indigestion, and the others have been influenced by his feeling.

I had hoped to strike a balance between work and relaxation and thus achieve results without loss of morale. It may be that I have expected a little too much, and have worked the boys too hard. Work for the mere sake of work was never reasonable to a boy. Yet idleness would be worse. Those who have tried it will tell you that nothing is more tedious than idleness. If one has leisure, he must fill it with something, even if that something is nothing more than another kind of work.

Camp Director Dawson arrived about an hour before lunch. We posted him on our progress to date and, at luncheon, he told us a good bear story.

It appears that in roping cattle, once the lasso has been thrown and the animal caught, the horse must do the

78

major part of the work, tightening the rope at the proper time, changing direction, standing, etc. Now, it is one thing to rope cattle, another to rope a bear, and it is a matter of pride among the cowboys to have a horse clever enough to handle bear properly. A cow when roped is likely to behave after a certain fashion, but a bear is different. He is liable to escape from the noose, and it takes a wonderfully trained horse to handle him.

Some time back there was a fellow in these parts who had a horse of which he was powerfully proud, and he decided to try him out on a bear. So he hunted up our canyon and, sure enough, one day he found a bear, which he promptly roped.

Everything was fine and the horse behaved perfectly until he happened to get a look at what they had roped, but this was enough to get him started off down the canyon on a run. The cowboy, figuring that the bear was taking pretty severe punishment, looked back, to discover that the bear was coming up the rope, hand over hand. This situation so alarmed him that he deserted the horse by the quickest method, sliding out of the saddle and leaving the horse and bear to shift for themselves. He had hardly had time to get his breath, and to wipe the dust out of his eyes, when he looked up to see how the horse was faring. To his amazement he discovered that the bear had mounted to the saddle and was riding down upon him.

"Mr. Dawson's stories were very good," wrote Bob, "and Chief was more than usually merry over them. I guess it was because they broke the monotony of our sour attempts."

The truth is that, in looking back, I am surprised to

79

have been recorded as "unusually merry" on the day when I was most concerned.

After lunch we went eastward down the canyon with Mr. Dawson as guide to look at some Indian writings. Wally took careful pictures for our expedition records while the rest of us explored the vicinity for village sites, but without success.

The commonest petroglyphs are carved in concentric circles, although there are some broken and arrowed lines, and a few pictographs of men and animals. The concentric designs are tantalizingly like targets and some of them had been used as such by passing cowboys.

The petroglyphs gave rise to a discussion of inscriptions in general. The boys had taken considerable interest in the subject en route to Philmont, reading the lines under the bust of many a local celebrity. Buttons, I remember, was especially impressed by the statues of the Pioneer Mother.

"I liked the Pioneer Mother with her two children and gun," he wrote. "They gave you a kind of respectful feeling. I guess the mothers never liked very much to leave home. They probably went because their men folks dragged them along.

"The boy was good, though, and lucky, too, to be a pioneer. My mother would worry if I went out with a gun. His must have worried if he went out without one. But mothers always worry. It helps to keep them busy."

The most touching inscription we could remember was that of an astronomer and his wife:

"We have loved the stars too fondly to be afraid of the dark."

80

Photo by Robert Butler

THE QUINNIPIAC SCOUTER
It carried us five thousand miles.

Photo by Norman Shemitz

THE LODGE AT FIVE POINTS
Without the lombardy poplar trees.

Photo by courtesy of *Scouting*

STATUE OF LUCIEN B. MAXWELL IN CIMARRON
It does not rain often enough to wash him away.

Photo by Wally Rubin

BILLY AND HIS OUTDOOR KITCHEN

He mixed biscuits with his "boot."

Photo by Norman Shemitz

BILLY WETSEL, OUR COWBOY

"We hold him in the light of a genius."

Photo by Wally Rubin

SALT LAKE CAVE
It is the dark spot under the tall dead pine.

Photo by Wally Rubin

BOX CANYON CAVE
It was home a thousand years ago.

INTERIOR OF BOX CANYON CAVE
It had been dry for centuries.

AN ARTIFACT IN PLACE
Irv excavates the woven section of a basket in Box Canyon Cave.

A SECTION OF THE WALL IN BOX CANYON CAVE
The Indians did some heavy work.

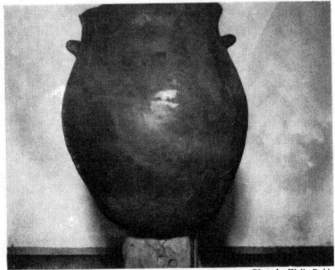

THE SALT LAKE CAVE POT RESTORED
It had been found in fragments.

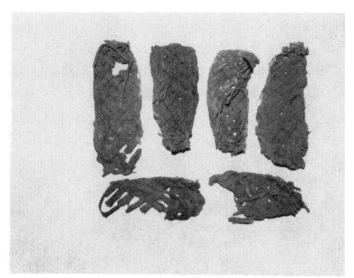

Photo by Wally Rubin

YUCCA SANDALS FROM BOX CANYON CAVE
They had been worn. The heels were run down.

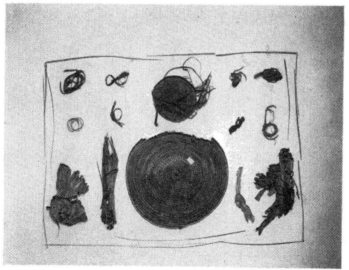

Photo by Wally Rubin

VEGETABLE ARTIFACTS FROM BOX CANYON CAVE
The Indians were good at knot tying.

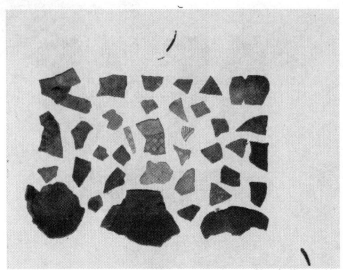

POTSHERDS FROM BOX CANYON CAVE
The black and white sherds were important.

A GROUP OF MISCELLANEOUS ARTIFACTS FROM
SALT LAKE CAVE
The inhabitants had corn on the cob.

PETROGLYPHS (INDIAN WRITINGS) NEAR OUR CAMP
Wally called "Hands UP!" and snapped the picture.

MORE INDIAN WRITINGS

The horse was only a few hundred years old.

Photo by Wally Rubin

TOOLS AND TECHNIQUE IN SALT LAKE CAVE
The soil is peeled off in horizontal layers.

Photo by Wally Rubin

INTERIOR OF BOX CANYON CAVE
The timbers might serve as a calendar.

ART, TOPS, AND BUTTONS AT WORK
The dust is our undoing.

BOB BUTLER AT CAMP

He specialized in rattlesnakes and mud fights.

"BUTTONS" EN ROUTE TO BLACK
JACK'S HIDE-OUT

He felt "attached" to his horse at the end of
the day.

WALLY AT BOX CANYON CAVE

He set the camera and took the picture himself.

THE WINDING RIVER FROM SALT LAKE CAVE
It ran deep in sunflowers.

THE MOUNTAINS OF OUR STAR
Looking westward from camp.

The most amusing, one from Louisiana; a full-length statue of the deceased, holding in his hands a marble scroll on which is faithfully reproduced his marriage license. It was his wife's final answer to the wagging tongues which had whispered that they had never been properly united in wedlock.

We began our journey westward from Sequassen, a wonderful Boy Scout camp in the foothills of the Berkshires. Deep in the woods there an unknown hermit lies buried and his epitaph is familiar to us all:

> I will rest peacefully,
>   No matter how long,
> If the pines will bend over
>   To sing the wind's song;
> If the birds and the chipmunks
>   Will play over me still,
> In the forest I loved,
>   Near the spring on the hill.

In the extreme southeast corner of the ranch there is an old adobe house built as a home by Kit Carson. It is dilapidated now but is scheduled to be restored as a point of special interest. Our inscription for it would read something like this:

KIT CARSON AT PHILMONT
    In building this house, he thought
he was making a home, but he was erecting a monument.

Jim Fitch, the big scout of all big scouts in these parts, informs me that down in Texas many an old-time cowboy eyed the advent of barbed wire and the fenced in

81

range with suspicion. They feared the day might come when you could stage a roundup within a fifty mile radius, and that an enclosed one. It gave them jitters and a first-rate case of claustrophobia to boot. That is why one of them insisted on this inscription:

> Let the cattle horn my tombstone down,
> And the coyotes call their kin;
> Let the hosses come and paw the mound,
> But don't you fence it in.

About midafternoon, following Mr. Dawson's directions, a map drawn in the dust, we took the trail to Box Canyon, and climbed down the dry waterfall at its head. Suddenly, there was a shout of excitement. We had found a four-roomed cliff dwelling over a hundred feet long! This was an archaeological discovery of the first magnitude.

But our survey was a bit discouraging. We were not the first. The cave had been dug in about half of its area by relic seekers, and rather generally disturbed.

Sizing up the situation, however, I decided that the best part, archaeologically, had been little disturbed. This is the accumulation of rubbish near the walls, and the outside talus. I noted also that the wall had fallen in several places, and I knew that if we were willing to move the heavy debris, we would be rewarded.

It was already late afternoon and we had, at best, only a couple of hours before dark in which to work. We set to feverishly, putting in temporary stakes, and starting immediately to excavate. We would do a thorough job of laying out the cave tomorrow, but today would be given to exploration.

82

Our first discovery was corn; cobs, shucks, and even a whole grain or two. Then, as our excitement mounted, we found some pieces of flint, potsherds, animal bones, and a brush made of pine needles. Art gave up digging in order to give his full time to cataloguing as our discoveries came in rapid succession: dozens of vegetable artifacts, two problematical bone tools, and a fine elk antler tool. Suddenly Tops cried out.

"Chief, look here!"

The tense quality in his voice was enough to bring us all quickly to his side. There, in the flaked dust, was the faint outline of a matted object, with a definite plaited pattern.

We laid aside trowels and shovels and taking a small wire brush began slowly and carefully to work around the object. Gradually it took form and, after several minutes, lay entirely revealed. It was a perfect sandal, even including the fiber tie.

Lifting it out carefully, we examined it with the greatest fascination. It had been worn. The heel was a little run down. Sometime, hundreds of years ago, its owner had climbed out of the canyon by the same route which had brought us in, wearing this identical sandal of woven yucca as protection against the rocks and briars. To look at the sandal, it might have been yesterday.

But one of the sherds is clearly black on white Pueblo, and that could not be yesterday. A ceramic sequence has been worked out for the Southwest, so that this one sherd is sufficient to establish the fact that our Indians lived here, shall we say, almost a thousand years before Keats wrote *Endymion*.

To have a cherished thought from a well-loved book come true in one's daily experience is one of the deepest joys of reading. It was not the sandal alone, or the sherd alone, but the whole setting of our afternoon's adventure, which brought *Endymion* to my mind:

A thing of beauty is a joy forever:
   Its loveliness increases; it will never
Pass into nothingness; but will keep
   A bower quiet for us, and a sleep
Full of sweet dreams, and health, and quiet breathing.

Before we came to the end of our daylight, Tops had discovered a refuse pit from which he kept pulling one thing after another. He was reluctant to leave it, and staked his claim to work it out tomorrow.

Meanwhile, Irv had cut some splendid tree-ring specimens from the beams in the wall, and Bob had unearthed an interesting corncob which had a skewer still stuck in the end. (This might be a prayer offering, or a simple convenience in handling.) The kernels of another corncob had been sliced off with a knife of some sort. This may have been evidence of succotash, a favorite Indian dish.

Art started his chart of the cave.

Wally and Buttons, having remained in camp in order to develop the pictures taken this morning, missed the excitement of this discovery, but they will be with us tomorrow.

Some of our discoveries seem incredible. We are finding corncobs, yucca fibers, pine needles, and such, because vegetable decay is contingent upon moisture, and the cave in which we have been working is dry, and

84

has been dry for centuries. If present conditions remain, as they almost surely will, these same artifacts might, if undisturbed, last for another thousand years.

We were so excited about the cave and our findings that we had not thought of eating. Consequently, we were late for supper, having allowed ourselves barely enough time to get off the mountain before dark. Billy mumbled a little about his biscuits being overdone, but was soon carried along on the wave of our enthusiasm.

He has only a polite interest in our archaeological work. We are alternately pleased or discouraged, depending upon our fortunes, but he will not worry about anything less important than the possibility of his horses running away, which they have done twice, or the texture of his precious sour-dough biscuits. I am reminded of a story about another native who, when queried about the work of certain archaeologists, replied: "Oh, all they did was to dig up a couple of putrefied skeletons."

But we will take Billy as he is. Like the juggler of Notre Dame, he is a simple man with no gift to astonish or amaze; yet beside the juggler, and before the altar of the Highest, Billy might present his sour-dough biscuits, warm and brown and fragrant. What need then of incense, spices from India, or cedars from Lebanon?

A hummingbird visited us, whirring his wings so noisily that Tops called him a bomber. We had already remarked upon the unusual number that occur here, obviously of several different species. The one we saw this afternoon had a brown head, brown and white speckled throat, white breast, brown wings, and green back. I felt a slight frustration at our inability to identify

85

it, and thought fondly of an honored friend of other years, Louis Agassiz Fuertes of Ithaca. "Uncle Louis," had he had the chance, could have painted our little bird from memory. As long as people live who remember Louis, there will be some to whom the birds are twice as beautiful.

Our little slump in morale is entirely over. The excitement of discovery and interesting work to do has restored all to new enthusiasm. We feel, for the first time, that our objective may actually be within reach, and that we may be able to tell a fair story of the prehistory of Philmont.

Late today I used the damp sands of our small river for a telephone pad and drew triskelia with a stick as I pondered our slight dip in morale. Suddenly I realized that it had probably had its origin in Tops's encounter with the barbed-wire fence. He has not been feeling quite normal because of a mild reaction to the antitetanus injection, and this may have been just enough to cause his discouragement.

Whitman would have loved this country! The grandeur of the mountains, the solitude, and the distances would have given him cause to underscore his famous words:

> Now I know the secret of the making of the
> best persons. It is to grow in the open air and
> to eat and sleep with the earth.

The Twelfth Chapter

FOR TOPS

My dear young friend:
  The best music is not somebody else's;
It is the sound
  And rhythm of your own living;
It is within you, and of your making,
  Always.
I know by ear that the best melodies
  Are those which you sing.

Thursday, August 28

WEATHER: Cloudy at 6:30 A.M. Showers later. Temperature 42° F.

CONDITION of Party: Partly shivering.

We had hopes of an early breakfast, but Wally, Buttons, and Bob loitered about getting up so that, in spite of Billy's anxiety to get started for Base, and our desire to get under way for Box Canyon, we did hardly better than usual. Wally and Buttons will have to go to bed at eight-thirty tonight to insure ten hours of good sleep and the spirit to rise when morning comes. I exempt Bob from this only because he is older, should and does know better, and doesn't actually need ten hours of sleep.

We normally sleep with our tent flaps rolled high, and we have no thermostatic control of our bedroom which, in effect, is the out-of-doors itself. This morning we could see our breaths and Prince and Dan, the horses, seemed to be exhaling steam. The cold may, of course, explain the reluctance of the boys to climb out from the warm comfort of their sleeping bags.

The interval between pajamas and warm clothing was chilly, and pimpled with goose flesh. These might be a reminder of a time when our bodies were covered with a more useful crop of hair, as each involuntary pimple is at the base of a hair follicle. Goose pimples are, I understand, the equivalent of an animal puffing out its fur,

88

or a bird fluffing its feathers against the chill winds. It is a kind of evolutionary hangover which does us no present good.

Our altitude is well over seven thousand feet and Mr. Dawson has warned that we might expect frost almost any morning, this time of year. So we must be prepared for almost anything, weather-wise. Some of the mountains within Philmont rise to twelve thousand feet.

Mr. Dawson told another story yesterday which is worth recording. There was, he reports, a civic-minded priest in one of the adjacent towns who was interested in everything which appeared to be for the general good of the community, and could always be counted upon to do his part.

When the time came when the Presbyterians were going to build a new church, however, there was some debate as to whether the Father should be approached for a subscription. Finally, it was agreed that he should not be left out, and two of the citizens volunteered to call on him.

The priest received them courteously and emphasized his desire to do any good thing for the community. But, he added, it seemed that helping to build a new Presbyterian church might be stretching the matter just a little.

"What are you going to do with the old church?" he inquired.

"Oh," the solicitors replied, "we are going to tear that down."

"Good," said the Father, rubbing his hands together. "You can put me down for twenty-five dollars toward tearing it down."

Our first job at Box Canyon Cave this morning was

to complete the task of staking it out in six-foot squares. Because of adjustments which had to be made to allow for walls and large boulders within the cave, this proved an extended job, and it was ten o'clock before we were ready to start digging.

Tops, Irv, Bob, Buttons, and I each took a section to work, while we kept Wally busy taking photographs, and Art with cataloguing.

The cave was so fertile that it would be tedious to list all the specimens found during the day. The principal ones included a fine square-toed sandal, several bone tools, numerous potsherds, and additional tree-ring specimens. There were also a small quartz arrowhead and two wooden implements which may have been used as pothooks, canes, or pokers.

There was considerable evidence of the eating habits of the former occupants of the cave: pinyon nuts, corn, pumpkins (we found seed), yucca, sunflower, wild plums, acorns, and a variety of animal bones including squirrel, deer, and elk, but no vitamin pills.

The corn is most plentiful. It has been reported that the Indians had more varieties than we have today. It was basic to their culture. Since they had no plows it was usually planted with digging sticks, and other vegetables were habitually planted wtih the corn, particularly such vegetables as squashes, pumpkins, and beans. The Indians had popcorn, too. All but the whistle.

The dust is our undoing. Digging involves a constant stirring and sifting of the soil which keeps it swirling. It envelopes us in floating geology, settling in our hair and on our clothes.

90

"The accumulation on the body gets wonderfully intense," said Tops. "I have an extra epidermis."

"Which you don't need," retorted Irv. "You are already thick-skinned."

The gauze masks serve very well but seem uncomfortable after an hour or two and we become conscious of breathing. We change masks several times a day. We stopped digging at three-forty-five and returned to camp for a bath and change of scenery.

As we climbed out of the canyon, Buttons slipped and fell, dropping a bag of our precious artifacts. Tops chided him for his carelessness but Buttons was quick-witted.

"Don't get so excited," he said. "I'll have twice as many of them."

Camp is now in excellent condition. We have been improving it every day, and now live in comparative luxury. The flies, while numerous, are not as bad as they were, and they always go to bed before we do and, on these chill mornings, do not rise earlier.

As we came down the trail this afternoon, we stopped for a few minutes to rest. After a while Irv said, "Let's go on home." It seemed a natural statement to us all and yet Irv revealed, unconsciously, the warm feeling we have for our camp. It is our home after the day's work. There is always some time to relax, to play in the river, write a letter home, or start some friendly game.

Billy's return from Base at five o'clock was the signal for all to rush for mail and the latest news from the folks back home. Our letters, which we receive whenever anyone happens to hike over the mountain, are about our only communication with the outside world.

Mine, received today, averaged over six days old, so that even these bulletins are on the late side.

During his absence Billy had invested in a haircut. It was so thorough that it caused some amusement among the boys, which Buttons recorded in his diary:

"Billy came back from civilization with his hair cut very short. Everyone was quiet until he took his hat off. Then we roared. Billy was a little put out and defended himself. 'A fellow has got to git the most for his money now-a-days,' he said.

"At supper, for the first time in all our meals, Billy messed up the soup. There were tons of pepper in it. Could it be his revenge?"

The day has continued cool with showers and a penetrating moisture in the air, so that we have built a comfortable fire in our fireplace.

"At such a time," I observed to the boys, "a campfire is good to look at, but more comfortable to back up to."

One useless bit of equipment frequently carried by boy scouts is a sheath, or hunting, knife. The scouts rarely have an opportunity to use one for any practical purpose, almost never for skinning an animal, which would be the commonest use to which a hunter might put it, yet they dearly love to go about with one hanging from their belts. A Pennsylvania scout hiked in from Base carrying two!

I suppose the chief satisfaction is a sense of being armed with a weapon of some potency, adding a touch which, in the imagination of a boy, is heavy with adventure.

Tonight my gang has found a use for them, and each

and every knife is being thrown at a tree, the object being to stick it in at some twenty feet. Not having been made for this purpose, points will be dulled and handles loosened, yet one will have his mythical championship as the best darn knife-thrower in Ponil Canyon. Button's knife, having gone wide of the mark and missed the tree entirely, is now being searched for with sticks and prods in a mud puddle left over from the afternoon showers.

Billy's spirits, which for reasons best known to himself had been low since his return from Base, rose during the evening as he described the complexities of breaking horses.

"Some of 'em," he said, "are just like some people, awful hard-headed. You teach 'em one thing one day, and the next day you have to teach 'em all over agin."

Prince had run away again during the night and Billy spent several hours looking for him.

"I hunted down canyon, not up," he explained, "because when a horse runs away, he always turns in the direction he was brought up."

"Suppose he was running away from the place he was brought up?" asked Wally.

Billy snorted.

"Who's goin' to run away," he said, "when he's got no place to run to?"

Billy himself is of the plains and mountains, of Texas and New Mexico, always of the rugged and sunburned country. But his broncho-busting days were interrupted by one magnificent adventure. During the First World War Uncle Sam sent him to Siberia.

"I near froze to death," he said, smilingly wryly.

Proudly, he showed us pictures of his wife and child.

We had delicious steak for supper, prepared strictly Western style, having been dipped in flour and cooked with lots of savory gravy. The idea of a rare steak makes Billy shudder. The Western custom of cooking meats so thoroughly may have come about because of a lack of refrigeration at a time when to eat rare meat was to risk contamination. Now the method is an art absorbed in custom, the preference as natural as pepper to a Mexican, beans to a Bostonian.

A noise is all right in its place. The scream of the hawk, the call of the jay, and the scold of the magpie are natural here. But the antiquated trumpet which Tops and Irv purchased in Carlisle, Pennsylvania, on our way West is another matter. It cost five dollars and belongs four-fifths to Tops, and one-fifth to Irv. It is, in the opinion of the rest of the fellows, five-fifths junk. There is an occasional clear note in a jumble of sour, but Tops feels that he is "keeping his lip in."

We do have music. An incidental snatch of song here and there, a whistled bar or two, the crackling of dry leaves under foot, the moving river, and the high clear notes of the rock wren, these have their melodies. But the wind is our best singer of songs, the wind in a chorus of trees.

Tops is an ardent Wagnerian. He is just as certain that Wagner is the world's greatest composer as he is that Poe and De Maupassant are the greatest writers of short stories.

It may be that Wagner is to the youthful musician what the *Rubaiyat* of Omar Khayyam is to the budding intellectual. The *Rubaiyat* is the first philosophy that is

94

simple enough for him to understand and, at the same time, sufficiently dangerous to be satisfying. I do not think the stanza about the "loaf of bread" and the "jug of wine" is the climax for the young reader. It is more likely to be one calling for more drastic action:

> Ah Love! could you and I
>   with Him conspire
> To grasp this sorry Scheme of
>   Things entire,
> Would we not shatter it to bits—
>   and then
> Re-mould it nearer to the Heart's
>   desire!

No doubt I shall be called to task for daring to infer that Wagner is as simple, musically, as the *Rubaiyat* is philosophically. I know better, of course. Wagner is more complicated. But the simple Omar, with his wily charm, matches Wagner in his way; a rose for a storm, a wineglass for a galloping Valkyrie.

Yet, I should defer to Tops. He will make his own music someday.

It is a night in which diurnal creatures must snuggle deeply into their burrows to escape the damp chill, and nocturnal prowlers will find mist in their faces and, unless they are very hungry, may return to their homes to wait for a change of weather. We are in the middle of a great dripping cloud which has settled in heavy quietness along the canyon floor. We have our burrows, too, and hardly more than a nose appears outside of the cosy bags in which the boys are sleeping.

There is, in the wilderness of our hearts, a haunting

touch of the primitive, a smouldering spark of kinship with our mother, Earth, which waits but a kindling breeze from out of our pasts to live again. Tonight it blows gently through Ponil Canyon, and I shall hesitate to close my eyes, lest I should lose it forever.

The Thirteenth Chapter

LULLABY FOR BIG BOYS *

In the warm blanket
  Whose folds are my heart,
Sleep Tops and Irving,
  Sleep Wally and Art.

CHORUS: *Under the stars, my sons,*
        Young dreams are kind;
        Only the willow waves
        Soft in the wind.

Sleep, Bob and Buttons,
  My blanket is warm;
It will enfold you
  And keep you from harm.

* To be thought, but not sung.
  Imagine singing my boys to sleep!

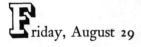riday, August 29

WEATHER: Slightly cloudy. Temperature at
6:30 A.M. 40° F.

CONDITION of Party: Excellent.

Faint discipline never made a seven-o'clock breakfast, and although I did not, officially, see Wally and Buttons dumped out of their sleeping bags, the continued chilly weather did not prove an obstacle to a prompt start for the dig this morning.

Our day, archaeologically, was very successful. Discoveries were numerous and included a woven basket, the bottom of a gourd which had been painted in concentric black circles, another sandal, bone implements, flints, an arrowhead, potsherds, and additional food clues.

We are finding bunches of knotted corn husks in abundance, almost invariably tied in a square knot, although some are overhand. The shucks may have been tied together for convenience in hanging them in storage, yet we are finding similar knots tied in other vegetable artifacts. Every scout knows that the square is about the best and simplest of all knots, and we were pleased to observe that the Indians used it. Some of the husks may have been turned back and knotted for convenience in roasting the corn. This practice has been reported among modern Indians.

We are finding quantities of shredded fiber, sometimes by the handful. The boys have advanced a number of

98

theories to explain its use, from tinder for making fire, to bedding. I am convinced that at least one batch of it was a rat's nest.

The discovery of a good refuse pit is a delight to the archaeologist. It may not have been very sanitary in its day but it was unconsciously historic. The same may be said of some of our modern dumps. They will be great places to visit in a few thousand years, and you will not have to hold your nose then.

In this cave there are a number of large boulders which were too big for the Indians to move, and the crevices between them formed excellent catchalls. Judged by the quantities of corncobs, husks, and general debris which we have found in them, they were used deliberately for waste disposal.

The use of the word "cave" in describing our site may be slightly misleading in that one often thinks of caves as dank and dark. Actually, visibility is good in Box Canyon Cave even during cloudy intervals. Perhaps our dig could be better described as a cliff house.

It is under an overhanging cliff which extends outward 37 feet at the widest part, and averages about 24 feet in width. Its length, from end to end, is 132 feet. The roof or overhanging cliff is 33 feet above the floor of the cave at the outer edge. It tapers back and downward rapidly, but there is adequate headroom until it reaches the innermost recesses.

"The rim of the canyon hangs over like a great protecting hand," said Bob, "as it must have been to the Indians."

The outer floor, beyond the dry wall, has a cover of small shrubs, but it is very dry on the inside. It is apparently impossible for natural moisture to penetrate the main dwelling. The cave faces approximately north, but the intervening trees, the opposite wall of the canyon, and the rising land beyond form an effective barrier against the cold winds, and must have been welcome protection when fierce winter whistled above the canyon rim.

Of the four divisions, or rooms, the east one is slightly higher than the rest and tends to be dampish. We doubt if it was lived in extensively, but think it may have served as a cool storage for foodstuffs. The next room is the largest and was, no doubt, the principal living quarters. The wall which divides this room from the east one terminates in a large boulder, short of the rear of the cave, thus forming a definite connection between the two rooms. The inner walls between the other rooms have fallen in places, so that we cannot be positive there were entrances between them. It is possible that the separation was complete and that more than one family occupied different ends of the cave at the same time.

The outside walls are intact in front of the east room and the main room, averaging here from eight to ten feet high. They are constructed of the same loose-grained stone from which the cliffs are formed and probably had fallen from overhead, so that there was no problem of transportation. The stones are tied with pine logs, upon which we have a jealous eye, as we know them to be the calendar which may date our findings. Although there is evidence of many fires, the ceilings of the cave are not badly discolored with soot. Perhaps the draft was good.

The Indians had at least two trails into the cave. The

100

first, down from the head of the canyon, was probably favored most of the time, especially in dry weather. It may have been risky during the rainy season. The second is up the cliff from the floor of the canyon, a hard climb at any time, which would of necessity have been preceded by a rugged hike up from the canyon's mouth. It is likely that other, man-made trails have been obliterated with time. We have seen no evidence of ladders, but I am confident that they had some, of sorts.

At the end of our working day Bob was busy with an interesting fire pit, Tops was working a fertile section, and Irv had just staked his claim in an area giving excellent indications. Meanwhile, I had found a splendid group of sherds which may go together and give the outlines of another pot.

Obviously we shall spend the remainder of our time on this dig, as there is still a great deal to do. We have not yet touched the talus, or the area immediately outside of the walls. We hope to do this much. The tempting explorations into the hills beyond will have to wait for other times, perhaps for other explorers.

It has been our custom to take lunch to the dig each day. Billy usually sends us off with a couple of sandwiches each, plus some cans of fruit juice, and individual cans of dessert such as fruit salad. We have been literally opening these cans with pick and shovel, but today the evil spell was broken. Billy included a can opener. We always crush and bury the empty tins after a meal. We are also a little sensitive about being "tin-can campers," but have no real reason to complain about our rationing.

A Connecticut scoutmaster and his scouts looked in on

our excavations, taking movies and snapping casual pictures.

"I've got several shots I want to use up, anyway," one of them explained.

I'm afraid they were too busy going places to see much. Travelers seem to divide into two main groups, the observers and the sight-seers. The observers store up an understanding knowledge of the places and things they have seen; the sight-seers are content with kaleidoscopic impressions and the fact of having "been there." One group is seeking knowledge, and the other is satisfied with a kind of background for bragging.

We are not camping for the mere sake of camping. We are, I am satisfied, doing an excellent brand of camping as a means to an end, rather than as an end in itself. We sleep in tents, eat meals which have been cooked over an open fire, excepting the tin-can lunches, wash our own clothes, and enjoy our evening fires. But mere camping would pall on one in time. We found one party of scouts who, having climbed a mountain, taken a ride on horseback, and looked at the scenery, decided that they had exhausted the possibilties of the West! They deserve stone blisters for the rest of their lives.

The best formula is not to go camping at all unless you have a purpose. It may be anything from a fishing trip to a scientific expedition, but it should be planned. Before leaving you should prepare: first, to accomplish the objective; and second, to camp comfortably. For best results you should take only those things which are necessary, lightening your pack of surplus equipment and your mind of extraneous thinking.

The first thing to do upon arrival is to establish a

well-ordered camp, in which each man's responsibilities are well defined. Having accomplished this, you may go on about your business of fishing or digging, and the camping will take glorious care of itself. If it doesn't, you will choose your companions more wisely next time.

Buttons took three tumbles during the day and I laughingly called him a tumbleweed. After the third he looked up at me with an embarrassed grin, for he had hurt himself. I gave no word of sympathy, although I think he understood my smile. He might appreciate being understood. I knew he did not want to be babied.

"A boy like that," remarked Billy, who had seen the last fall, "what can take the bumps and git up and go on about his business without sayin' nothin', would go a long way in this country."

Following Bob's bath in the creek, he came up naked and glistening, a statuesque young godling fit to be sculptured. But he had forgotten to wash his face, which was streaked and caked with dust. Unwilling to slide down the slippery bank again, he went mumbling to the pump.

After supper Billy, with Prince as his victim, demonstrated how to throw the lariat. Prince, a tolerant but obviously unhappy horse, eyed us reproachfully.

"Look at him," said Billy, "pretendin' his feelings are hurt."

Tops learned, also from Billy, how to blow First Sergeant's Call on the trumpet, plus an unprintable interpretation of its meaning. Billy knew the meanings of all the calls. He had not been to Siberia for nothing.

Tops and Irv both have unkempt and smudgelike upper lips as the result of an attempt to grow mustaches.

103

"You see," commented Billy to me, "how anxious they are to be men. If they could really grow mustaches, they wouldn't care, but now!"

"Will they be satisfied to be men?" I asked him.

Billy looked at me, suspecting some hidden meaning in the question.

"You mean me to answer that?"

I nodded.

"Sometime, when they grow up," he said, "they may feel like cryin' because they aren't boys agin. But they will always want to be men."

I was silenced by his wisdom.

Art badly needs a shave, too. He has never had one and, although the possibility has been suggested to him, he intimates that the first shave is a ceremony which he wishes to save for a time when he will be surrounded by his admiring family.

The boys have enjoyed the lizards. The two common ones, the swift and the blue-tailed skink, both occur here; the swift in abundance, and perhaps the skink also. The swift, by description of the boys, has a "herringbone design," while the skink "has a pattern like a garter snake."

Bob captured a swift and described it in his notes:

"He is a spirited little lizard about four inches long, and his tail is as long as his body. He is rock-colored for protection, but his bottom-side is vivid blue."

After hiking down the trail in the moonlight he stopped at my tent to say good night.

"Chief," he said, "the moonlight is so bright that down on the trail I can count the shiny eyelets in my sneakers.

This gives me a comparison for all moonlight nights in the future."

"It's wonderful, Bob," I said. "Good night."

"Good night, everybody," I called. "Pipe down and sleep."

I had been thinking of Thomas Mann's *Joseph in Egypt*, and of the melodious ways in which the young Joseph said good night. One should have soothing words at the end of the day, to drift to sleep in comfort and quiet peace. I depended upon the friendliness of my voice to convey what Joseph might have said:

"Ride happily in the great Rodeo of Dreams, my sons, and may the morning give you cause for smiling."

The Fourteenth Chapter

HUNTER'S SONG

Tread softly in the wilderness
  If you would learn its ways,
Your greatest skill is quietness
  And a song of praise.

CHORUS: *Praise for the distant hills and sky,*
        Praise for the silver rain,
        Praise for the river winding by,
        And praise for the fertile plain.

Go softly into the wilderness,
  Silently and slow,
The hunter's skill is quietness,
  And his voice is low.

Saturday, August 30

WEATHER: Fair. Temperature at 6 A.M. 46° F.
Much warmer during the day.

CONDITION of Party: Unrecorded.

Buttons demonstrated for me, quite unconsciously, the process through which the human animal goes when waking from sleep. I shook his sleeping bag, and he burrowed into his pillow and stuck his chin down between his humped-up shoulders. I shook again, and he opened one eye tentatively, then squinted at me from both, half opened. There followed a series of noisy yawns which he grumbled out while scratching his tousled hair, then, stretching his arms over his head, he explored his full length, arching his back and stretching from toes to fingers. Grunting, he lowered his arms back into the sleeping bag, pulled up his pajama bottoms, and hitched out on his elbows. Sitting up in bed, he fisted his eyes, digging the morning sand out of the corners with the third finger of his right hand, blinked again and said, "Mornin', Chief."

Sliding his feet off the cot, he fumbled them into his moccasins, stood up, walked to the door of his tent, and, clearing his throat lustily, spit the taste of sleep out of his mouth. Then he glanced at the sky, and made a bee-line for the latrine.

At breakfast Billy told us about the native farmer who grew pumpkins on the side of a mountain so steep that

108

he used a shotgun to plant the seeds and later employed the same means to sever the vines so that the pumpkins would roll downhill to be harvested.

That reminded us of another story about the rock-ribbed hills. It appears that a motorist was driving along the highway when he had suddenly to jam on his brakes as a farmer landed in the road in front of him. The farmer got up, brushed himself off, and apologized.

"That's the second time I've fallen out of that gol-darned field this morning," he said.

Our reputation for promptness has improved, and we were busy with our excavations at Box Canyon Cave by eight-fifteen this morning. We dug two additional sections to sterile soil during the day, accumulating considerable additional material.

Irv, through a combination of good luck and untiring energy, remains our best discover. In one exciting cache this morning he unearthed a sandal, a woven basket, numerous potsherds, and various vegetable artifacts. He has a way of finding things while the others are resting.

Bob had fun excavating a fireplace which had been built of stones. He thought he could figure out its plan of ventilation. In the same section Art found a fine arrowhead about an inch and a half long. This is the only one of this size we have found, the others being characteristically much smaller. A few fragments of turquoise were the sensation of the morning.

"Well," said Tops, "our Indians weren't quite paupers, after all."

"Maybe they had a lot of it," offered Bob, "because they would have taken it with them when they left."

The turquoise, according to legend, is a delicate and

109

sensitive jewel having an affinity with its owner which causes it to vary in color with his health and changing fortunes. The fact that it does change color might easily contribute to such a superstition.

They were sacred to the royal house of Montezuma, and four of them were among the first presents sent to Cortez. "A gift," recorded Bernal Diaz, "designed as a mark of highest respect, as each of them, they assured us, was worth more than a wagonload of gold."

In addition to sandals made of yucca, we have found evidence of a much wider use of this plant. Some authorities maintain that yucca ranked foremost among the wild economic plants of the Southwest, having been to the desert Indian what the date palm has been to the Arab. The fruits, flowers, and crowns were used for food, and the fibrous leaves were made into thongs, sandals, matting, basketry, cloth, nets, straps, cradles, brushes, and related objects. The roots contain a soapy material useful for washing. Indeed, one may only surmise the extent to which the plant was used. Yet, as a food, it did not compare with the cultivated maize or Indian corn.

After lunch we began excavations in the talus, or accumulated residue of dirt and rubbish in front of the cave, and at four o'clock this afternoon, when we stopped for the day, Tops had begun to turn up sherds in that area.

We were delighted with the arrival, just before noon, of Rodney Cobb, who came down the trail riding the horse, Buck, and guided by Mr. Dawson. Rod had won the boys completely during our stay in Norman, and the welcome he received was a genuine tribute.

Mr. Dawson remained with us for a while and endeavored to help us find a metate, or grinding stone, which is known to have been in the site, but is now missing. Mr. Dawson, who had seen it, described it as about thirty inches long and twelve inches wide, with a lengthwise groove through the center. The description is of a typical metate which would fit into the rest of our discoveries. Apparently it has fallen to souvenir hunters ... and, I hope, on their toes.

We explored the territory above the north bank of the canyon during the afternoon and found flint chips on the slope of the near-by knoll. Rod pointed out shinny oak, a dwarf variety which grows to an average height of only four feet or so, yet bears a robust acorn. It is common here.

There is an equally interesting shrub known as Ponil bush, or lemonade plant, which has been named for this canyon. It is a glossy aromatic sumac which grows to about six or eight feet in height and bears a spicy citrus berry which is favored by the natives, who maintain that it gives relief from thirst.

In a discussion of the aromatic, one should not forget the common sagebrush. It is a spicy member of the aster family and, in climbing, one will take hold of it in preference to a more prickly plant. Your reward is a nose-tickling wave of spicy fragrance.

Rod is an expert in laboratory and field techniques and, just before supper, demonstrated to the boys a method of taking plaster casts of the petroglyphs. With their new knowledge they proceeded immediately to cast the one petroglyph which seems likely to be spurious.

We have placed some premium on wit and humor, and our normal standard is fairly high. Art is very clever at puns, and Irv is a good mimic. Sometimes, too good. But for the moment the boys have lost perspective as between real humor and plain silliness. There is an epidemic of reiterations, especially of phrases and tones of voice, and nothing can be more tedious than repeated witticisms. Buttons has the best score. He has not copied the others, or repeated himself.

The sunset changed the river into a stream of copper and gold, and Irv attempted to capture it with his camera and color film. The cloud effects were magnificent. There should have been cloud worshipers among the Indians of these canyons, for the clouds are irresistibly beautiful. Deep in the past the primitive red man may have wondered if these were not, indeed, the robes of the Great Spirit, the Most High.

There was much cowboy talk around the chuck fire. Billy smoked one of Rod's cigars, while Rod and I "rolled our own" with his Bull Durham tobacco for a filler. Billy and the cigar did not appear to go well together. He smoked it incongruously, and the boys giggled without knowing why. But they laughed heartily at my attempts to roll a good homemade cigarette.

I gave Rod my bed and slept on the ground.

"I suppose you think you are as tough as a boot heel, as they say out here," he remarked.

"Oh, I'll hardly be able to tell the difference," I replied. But I lied.

In the quiet interval before sleep Rod quoted from his chief, Dr. Clements of the University of Oklahoma:

"Man stands on the shores of an ocean of knowledge, where truths are cast as bright pebbles upon which he gazes in childlike wonder, and all of these intimations of a wider world...he uses as the playthings of the moment."

I liked that. It sounded poignantly true. Yet many of those pebbles seem brighter and more glistening while they are still wet down there on the beach. If you should gather a bucketful and carry them home, you might find upon arrival that you had carried only a weight of common stone. And if those pebbles were as the sands of your life, how many could you choose, knowing them still to be the clear and shining truth?

The Fifteenth Chapter

FOR RODNEY

I have been seeking greatness all my life;
    The quest is fruitful, though it fails the best.
I do not look for smallness, and that knife
    Cuts deeper for its unexpectedness.

But you are like the sun on sparkling days,
    Accenting beauty with its clear, cool light;
There is an understanding in your ways,
    And wisdom, which is greatness, in my sight.

Sunday, August 31

WEATHER: Fair. Temperature at 7 A.M. 58° F.

CONDITION of Party: Thoughtful.

We enjoy a sociable breakfast. This morning Rod was the raconteur. There was a professor, he told us, whose custom it was to enter his classroom through a door leading directly to the rostrum, and of making a formal exit by the same route. One morning, in preparing to leave, he tripped and fell forward into the lecture room. The students roared. The professor picked himself up, glared at the class, and stated haughtily:

"I have given many lectures, but this is the first time I have descended to the level of my audience."

We started for the dig immediately after breakfast. Our first problem was to ford the river, and all were prepared for wading except Rod. He was traveling light and had not brought boots. Tops and Art volunteered, by locking their hands and wrists together, to form a chair-carry and take him over. This seemed picturesque to Buttons, who decided to take a picture of it. Looking at the little stream, and studying the shutter openings on his camera, he inquired:

"Shall I set the camera for a marine scene?"

This remark struck our camera-wise party as delightfully naïve.

"See if it has an opening for brains," Irv suggested.

At the dig we excavated three additional six-foot sec-

116

tions, but concentrated on our test trench through the talus. This trench did not reveal much beyond a few chips and sherds, but we felt that proper technique required that it be dug. It was a task of the first magnitude, requiring the removal of many large stones which had fallen from the wall and been buried in the detritus of hundred of years. Artifacts discovered during the day were similar to those already recorded, the exception being one fine stone bead.

Rod was a valuable advisor. He made helpful suggestions throughout the day, and gave Wally particular assistance in the composition of pictures to be taken. His presence re-emphasized the importance of our task in the minds of the boys so that each worked with increased zeal.

"I wish we had time to hunt some of the mountain lions," one of them remarked to him.

"We are more fortunate," said Rod. "We are seeking knowledge in the form of adventure. Perhaps it is even a greater adventure than shooting lions. We have, in this cave, an indication of man's prodigious effort to improve himself. I think it has always been hard work."

At two o'clock we headed back to camp. On the way down the mountain I tasted the bitter weed *Helenium tenuifolium*, but will take the name for the deed any other time. It took twenty minutes of spitting and spewing to get rid of the acrid taste. No wonder that cows which feed upon it yield a witches' brew of bitter milk.

The mountain slopes are adorned with wild flowers: a lavender and a white aster, the yellow blossoming bitterweed, the Indian paintbrush, and a spiked lobelia. The purple lupin and scores of other spring species have

117

passed the blossoming stage. We see the inevitable goldenrod.

Billy had taken special pains in honor of our guest, and our meal was unexpectedly elaborate. During the meal Rod, who had glanced through my journal, expressed the belief that Clyde Malone was right about the sunflowers having increased after the dust storms, and that there is no doubt that vegetation in adjacent areas is influenced by such phenomena. He also mentioned the tepee circle at Base Camp, which he has not seen. He suspects it may have been a burial pit or some kind of ceremonial area.

We devoted the entire afternoon to Rod, taking as much advantage as possible of his short stay. He checked restorative techniques with Art and Buttons, petroglyphic pictures with Wally, and helped sift our entire collection of specimens. Altogether, we had a busy afternoon.

At six-thirty Rod said good-by and rode out from our camp and over the mountain. Here was one who loved scholarship with the devotion and fervor of a mediaeval monk dedicated to God. His departure left us keenly aware of our loss in not having had him as a full-time member of our expedition as originally planned. His brief impact on the boys had been lasting. We saw him go with regret.

Three species of cactus are familiar to this area, the pear, the barrel, and the tree, each being named for its shape. The pear and the barrel are common here, but we are not quite in range of the treelike species. We found ancient cactus in the cave, which is not surprising, as it is known to have been an Indian food.

Irv has suggested that the members of our party will not be thoroughly initiated into the mysteries of the Southwest until each has sat on a cactus. Tonight's inventory reveals that all have been initiated, one to the extent of five times.

"Instead of 'look before you leap,'" said Irv, "out here it is look before you sit."

In the late afternoon, with the sun behind the mountains, a graceful hawk hunted low above the sunflowers. He was wise to hunt in the shade where his shadow could not give alarm to his prey. A predator, before every meal he must satisfy the thrill of the hunter.

Art has usually recorded his day in about one sentence. Today he took several.

"Sunday, but no rest for the wicked. Worked up a good appetite, and needed it for the big dinner Billy cooked up. Mr. Cobb checked our specimens before he left. He was a swell fellow even if he was smart. Dan and Prince skipped out again, but Billy brought them in. He really likes those horses. The horses looked like two boys caught in the jam. Wally gave his face an extra washing, but it wasn't his fault."

It is late now. In a few minutes it will be September, and with the passing of August one senses that summer, too, is gone. The morning chill will reach deeper into the marrow, and we shall be off to our pleasant homes in the East. Happily, we came, and happy shall depart, yet not without the sadness one feels at the passing of something that was great and now is gone.

This last glimpse of August... the gently waving shadows of the graceful willow above my tent, cast by moonlight in changing patterns against my canvas wall.

The Sixteenth Chapter

We have buried our seven names,
  Under the dust, beneath the ruined wall;
Beyond the bitter winds of winter storms,
  In a dwelling place where no rains fall.

If, when a thousand years have passed,
  Our names are found, before they fade,
They will be as arrowheads, knots of grass,
  Or sandals that the Indians made.

We shall have gone with our laughter,
  Beyond the reading of our names.
Tomorrow may be ours; the day after,
  Our children's children stake the claims.

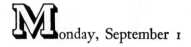

Monday, September 1

WEATHER: Slightly cloudy. Temperature at
7 A.M. 45° F.

CONDITION of Party: In need of a hot bath.

Following custom, I had a cup of hot coffee with Billy before signaling the boys to get up. This is an early-morning ceremony in which Billy and I share the weather lore of the morning and discuss briefly the problems of the day. It is a quiet period, given to low voices and unhurried pace. The hot coffee burns a spiraling hole of steam in the frosty air, but not for long. It is too good to delay drinking. Billy asserts that there is no substitute for it and, taking a second cup thoughtfully, I agree.

I have no need of my watch mornings. Billy's pan rattlings and wood snappings wake me, and I call the boys when the sun first strikes the mountains opposite. It is then, as I know from experience, just before seven o'clock.

At breakfast the boys talked about rattlesnakes. They are disappointed because they have not seen many, and expressed the hope that they might meet some on the way to the dig. They envy Bob, and would like to carry rattles home as souvenirs.

Billy asked if we knew how the snakes like to watch their rattles.

"They sure are proud of 'em," he stated sagely, and

122

proceeded to describe the proud rattler sunning himself on a rock while keeping an affectionate eye on his rattles as he moves them gently back and forth.

This homely observation brought to mind a rare bit of birdlore which an acquaintance in Louisiana acquired through observing the mockingbird.

The mockingbird, as all who know him will remember, has a habit of frequently lifting his wings as he walks or hops across the lawn. The wings are lifted in a quick stretching movement as if they were ill-fitted and needed to be readjusted. It is the kind of motion a man might make if he had on a shirt which was uncomfortable under the arms. The gesture is so characteristic of the mockingbird that he might almost have a patent on it.

But why? My friend wanted to find out. So he watched the birds until he discovered the reason. The wings are lifted in order to alarm small insects which, seeing the motion, take flight. This enables the mockingbird to see the insect, catch it, and proceed with his dinner. I checked these observations myself and found them accurate, yet have not encountered this fascinating bit of birdlore in any book.

My friend was a character. He was fond of birds in a locale so rich in them that they are neglected or taken for granted. But he watched them for hours at a time. By stealth and subtlety he introduced into his garden, under the guise of rare shrubs, a wealth of fruit and berry-bearing weeds and trees.

His wife, who loved her garden more, was never quite sure which plant might be an ornamental shrub or which a weed, so she patiently awaited the outcome of his transplantings, knowing the odds against her.

"But that pokeberry is a beautiful shrub!" he would protest, and when she pointed out another weedy specimen, he would argue its merits just as staunchly. The feud went on between them the whole year around, as the birds sang in their garden.

This is our last day at the cave. We decided to finish the sections started yesterday, and to dig a little more in the talus for a definitive treatment. The specimens discovered were such as are already familiar to us, although Irv found another good bone awl. By eleven o'clock we were finished, the cave policed, and preparations made for a return to camp.

As a final act each member of the party signed one of the long corner stakes which we had been using to lay out our digs, and this was driven deep under the wall as a record for future archaeologists who may decide to re-excavate. It may never see the light of day again and, in this dry place, may last longer than the memory of any other thing we have ever done.

We do not maintain that we have taken everything from this dig, but we believe we have collected sufficient, and representative, material from which to reconstruct in reasonable detail the life of its ancient inhabitants. The sections which we dug were taken to sterile soil and the artifacts left in them, in the main, only those of which we had adequate specimens of similar nature. Our material is to be presented to Peabody Museum at Yale University upon our return.

Standing at the canyon's mouth, I looked back into the cave, perhaps for the last time, remaining incredulous before the truth...that people had lived there; been conceived, born, had grown up, fought, worshiped, and sickened to death beneath that overhanging cliff.

It seemed pleasant enough for a picnic, and a good shelter from the summer showers. It might have been a proper refuge for the hunter in biting weather, to rest, and warm his hands, or roast his rabbit above a sheltered flame. But it had been more than all these. It had been home.

It had been the place to which the children returned after their games, the women from the crops and pinyon trees, and the men from their hunting. I do not doubt they had the same delight that we do when, weary from wandering, we turn toward the place which, above all others, is our home.

When to their gods they lifted their thoughts in supplication, it was for this rugged shelter that they prayed, this place of refuge from the heat and cold, this poignant bit of home. They lie buried now, somewhere in the hills near by, still at home in their mountains. They will not follow when we wade the winding river.

We are spending the afternoon in the numerous small tasks which must always be done toward the end of an expedition of this sort. Tops and Irv are mapping the canyon areas which we have explored, Art is reducing the charted drawings of Box Canyon Cave to India-ink copies, Wally finishing his photography, and Bob and Buttons assembling specimens for the journey out. We expect to complete all of these tasks this afternoon and be ready for an early start back to Base tomorrow.

These last few days have seen considerable scurrying around for souvenirs. Irv will take out the antlers of a deer, Art has an awl which he has fashioned from deer's bone taken from Box Canyon Cave, Buttons a horseshoe originally worn by Prince, Tops a collection of flint chippings, Bob some flint and cactus, and Wally an unnamable collection of small things. The horseshoe was his prize specimen, but Buttons gave me a complete list as follows:

> 1 horse shoe off of Prince
> 100 & 1 odd pieces of chips, etc.
> 1 perfect small arrow head—pint size
> 1 not so perfect arrow head
> 1 odd assortment of post cards
> 1 odd assortment of napkins
> 3 bars of perfumed soap
> 1 hunk of lava from Mt. Capulin
> 3 menus
> 1 do-not-disturb card
> A lot of other miscel. things

"This list is subject to change without notice," he concluded, "as I am always picking up unspeakables."

We held a brief council and the boys agreed unanimously that they wished to give Billy, our cowboy, a regular Western-style Stetson hat in appreciation of the splendid care he has taken of us. Billy is, without doubt, the real prototype of the cowboy and he has added greatly to the charm of our camp in the mountains, just by being himself.

Tops has long hankered for a coat of many colors. I remember once he thought of a blue and gold cape to drape, with seeming carelessness, across his shoulders. This summer his envious thoughts have dwelt upon a vest of rattlesnake skins! Irv and I have not attempted to conceal our amusement, but Tops remains impervious in his desire.

With Billy's connivance, we have created a mythical cowboy who has such a vest, made from twenty-seven skins! Tops talks in subdued tones about this marvel and has some temptation to use Billy as a go-between, as the missing cowboy hates Easterners "because they ask too many questions."

But we never seem to catch up with that cowboy. He has either just left Cimarron, or is in Raton, or is headed back toward some distant ranch. Tops does not know that the vest exists only in the happy hunting grounds of his own mind.

We had a final campfire in front of the great rock, with the story of Ticonderoga to end the day, and thus have come to our last night "on location." I am satisfied. A great deal remains to be done before the scientific story of our expedition can be told, but this promises interesting hours ahead.

I realize that the archaeology has not been as important as the experience. Within the sanctuary of these mountains we have found a slightly wider and nobler horizon, and I will not ask or hope for more, on this deep and final night, when our little river is running clear under the harvest moon.

The Seventeeth Chapter

I must say good-by to the willow,
  And the small winds that blow,
Over the wild sunflowers,
  Like music that I know.

Farewell to the wind and the willow;
  Tomorrow brings the snow;
The present soon becomes the past,
  And the past is long ago.

Tuesday, September 2

WEATHER: Fair. Temperature at 6:30 A.M.
45° F.

CONDITION of Party: Well tempered.

The boys rose at five-thirty to climb the mountain for the sunrise. Irv awakened me with an invitation to accompany them, but I had been up late with this journal and with the records of the expedition, so turned over for another hour of sleep.

They invited Billy, too, but he answered, "I ain't crazy yit," and passed up the opportunity. When I joined him for a cup of coffee about an hour later, he remarked, "I reckon it will take about forty years to tire them out."

They returned at seven o'clock as hungry as pack rats, but enthusiastic about their early-morning climb. Wally had a fall but, explained Tops, "He landed where he usually is, sitting down, so he wasn't hurt much."

"I almost fell off the same cliff," said Buttons, "but by luck I fell over a little tree instead of on solid nothing."

Perhaps it was fortunate we had so much to do in preparation for breaking camp and that there was no time for solemnity. Personal and expedition baggage had to be packed, tents taken down, latrine and garbage pits filled, and camp given a general policing.

We had the satisfaction of leaving the site in excellent

130

condition. In camping, cleanliness is the first virtue, and one has no right to the title "good camper" unless he practices it. Not once have I had to tell the boys to clean up their quarters, and they have hardly been conscious of my daily inspections. Camp health and happiness are often measured by cleanliness and order, and in these qualities my lads deserve an excellent rating.

Billy hated to leave the enormous gray squirrel which he had been feeding daily and which had become a virtual pet of the camp.

We left a little after nine o'clock for the hike over the mountain to Base Camp at Five Points, wading our little river for the last time, and mounting skyward gradually. The grasshoppers, invariable to our trails, whirred out of our passage, a hummingbird paused before us, motionless in his flight, and a lone buzzard coasted on the winds above.

Panting with the short breath of climbing in high altitudes, we stopped at the crest, our vision extended to a hundred miles of mountains. Hard, but rewarding work, it brought us at noon to the familiar haven of Base Camp, rustic and strong, yet seeming to us, who had seen neither house nor landscaped ground for many days, like civilization.

In our estimation the best symbol of this civilization was the hot shower! We reveled in lather and warm water, emerging at last with that delicious feeling of cleanliness which is one of the subtle marks of civilized man.

In the afternoon we boarded the Quinnipiac Scouter and went to Cimarron to buy a Stetson hat for Billy. The proprietor of the general store, we had been informed, had just acquired a new pony of which he was very proud. If, it was hinted, we were sufficiently enthusiastic about the new pony, it might have a favorable effect upon our purchase.

As luck would have it, we saw the horse, a fine tan and white pinto, just before we entered the store.

"A beauty," said Buttons, "a fugitive from a paintbox!"

We found the proprietor and won his heart immediately through our unbounded admiration for his pony. When it got down to the business of our purchase, he gave us a 25 per cent discount on Billy's Stetson without batting an eyelash.

I departed with the hat and a guilty conscience, but the boys reassured me.

"After all," they said, "what we told him was the truth. It is a fine horse, and besides, Billy needs the best hat that we could buy."

Be that as it may, if I ever get back, and the good merchant of Cimarron once again asks me to speak before his businessmen's club, I shall be in no position to refuse.

We gave Billy the hat at supper amid great good fellowship. I will let Buttons describe the incident:

"Billy once told Chief he preferred a black hat for practical reasons:

1. It would never have to be cleaned.
2. It gives a 'dapper' look to the wearer.
3. It sheds the glare of the sun better than a lighter shade.

132

"But there wasn't a black one of the proper size in Cimarron, so we bought a brown one instead. When we gave him the hat Billy was very happy and he gave us a little speech accompanied by the roar of the workmen, who already wanted to try it on.

"Billy readily became accustomed to the brown hat and strutted around in the most fashionable style."

Meanwhile, we presented our best archaeological shovel to Philmont as a souvenir and as evidence of our loyalty. It hangs now among the trophies in the main lodge at Five Points.

There is coal in these hills. We observed a few shafts on the route between Cimarron and Base Camp, although surface indications did not suggest commercial quantities. I am informed that some of the natives mine their own private supplies. An inferior vein strikes through the formation northwest of the lodge.

On the trip over the mountain this morning we remarked upon the universality of the protective device in the vegetation of this rugged and semiarid country. The weeds grow bitter, or strongly aromatic, or put forth spines. There is usually a brilliant flower to tempt the pollenizing insect, and a bitter taste or vicious spine to repel all others.

Bob gave the following description of one of the many stick-tights, or beggar lice:

"The land is grown up with small clumps of bushes that always seem to prick you one way or another. One type gave off small seeds that were actually shaped like arrows. They were about an inch long with a head that resembled the fore part of a bolt. But the part that got me was that the other end had small fibrous parts stick-

133

ing out that looked exactly like the feathers of an arrow."

We are billeted once more in the Scouters' Lodge, with a fire in the fireplace, and friendly visitors in the evening. Our friends the carpenters came to see and to admire our specimens.

The stars seem to peep over the mountains into this narrow valley, and it is easy to imagine that one could see it better from Arcturus or Vega than from any place on earth. Let no one have the faith to move these mountains. They belong where they are, framing the clouds by day and the stars by night, guarding this happy valley for our sons.

The Eighteenth Chapter

Sunset on Sangre de Cristo,
  Oh, poignant blood of Christ!
Let the rains pour tomorrow;
  I cannot bear to see you twice.

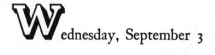

Wednesday, September 3

> WEATHER: Fair, with decorative clouds. I
> forgot to check the temperature.
> It felt just right.
>
> CONDITION of Party: In a new element.

We found a night's rest on mattresses an agreeable
change from the canvas tarps of Ponil Canyon. Though
we had no regrets for the pleasant hardships of our
canyon camp, we had gained added respect for a few
common conveniences such as mattresses and running
hot water.

Our breakfast at six-fifteen was not too early as we
had a big job of packing to do, which included sorting
all of our belongings and preparing a portion of them
for shipment home by express.

We had engaged horses for the day and were due
to report at the corral at nine o'clock. Tops and Irv
fretted a little for fear we might not be on time, and I
discovered later that they had optimistically moved the
time of our appointment at the corral an hour ahead!
Unfortunately, the packing had to be done and when
we "finally" arrived at the corral, it was nine o'clock.

With Red, another cowboy, as guide, we started on
the eighteen-mile trip to Black Jack Ketchum's hide-out
and return. I rode the reliable and sure-footed horse
Buck.

So far as Red was concerned it was a kind of "Follow

136

the Leader" without being a game. He was so taciturn and expressionless that I visualized him as an excellent companion for the late Calvin Coolidge. I estimated that one dictaphone record might last him for a season and, when transcribed, would read something like this:

"Yes."

"No."

"This way."

"Whoa!"

"That way."

"No."

"Yes."

"Git-ap!"

I thought to trap him into talking by asking about Black Jack's story.

"Just an outlaw," he replied, defeating me in three words.

It was a memorable day. Horseback riding is an adventure in itself, and our trip over the mountains was not an ordinary canter. En route we startled eleven deer, a porcupine, and numerous smaller animals.

The deer and the chickadee are the most moving lyrics of the forest. The deer is the most alert, with hardly a nibble that is not interspersed with a lifted head and watchful eye. The faint, unfamiliar crackling of a twig will send him bounding, yet his insatiate curiosity will bring him back again, and he is adaptable enough when once satisfied of his safety.

I have known deer to graze serenely beside a friendly camp, and while we were at Indian Writings two drank from the river there within a hundred yards of our camp, without alarm.

The chickadee has charm and grace out of all proportion to his size and importance. There is a twinkling flavor of merriment about him and he is a tease, perching nearly upside down on a branch almost as delicate and graceful as himself. To watch this animated bit of feathered acrobatics is to feel faintly amused at the whole world, and that is not a bad situation to be in.

Black Jack's hide-out proved to be a rather small cliff shelter such as earlier Indian parties may have used. A small stream furnished a trickle of water. With plentiful game in the adjacent hills a man might survive indefinitely.

We remained for lunch, sharing our crusts with the blue jays, who repaid us with raucous noises and excited callings. We had only to be reasonably quiet to tempt them to light on the rocks within a few feet, snatch the crumbs, and fly off. Whenever one made off with some of the food the others followed, squawking loud and bloody murder.

We have become well acquainted with those ostentatious birds, the magpies, too. Their striking black and white bodies and long tails give them a spectacular appearance as they fly, slowly and gracefully, their plumage flashing like a pirate's flag against the sky.

The magpie's reputation, like the jay's, is unsavory. Stealing, torture, and cannibalism are among the indictments against him, but even his enemies admit that he is smart. The nest is often built, for protection, in a thorn tree, roofed with sturdy twigs, and with a side entrance. It is very large, sometimes, according to ornithologists, the size of a barrel!

The commonest butterfly here appears to be a white

138

one, which I had been assuming was the familiar cabbage butterfly so well known in the East. But, today, looking down upon him from horseback, I discovered that he is embroidered with black spots on the fringes of the wings and is a new acquaintance.

"The ride," wrote Buttons, "was over hills and dale and sometimes dangerous steep paths. I almost got seasick but managed to keep from going overboard.

"On the way back I had trouble convincing my horse that maybe I should do the steering. He acted as though he knew more than I did, and I guess about this country he did. When we got back I was so stiff I was practically attached to my horse but, with an effort, I succeeded in getting off."

But the mountains were the real show, particularly the Sangre de Cristo, Blood of Christ, Range, snow-capped in the distance. They are so named because in winter when the snows cover them widely, the glow of the sunset reflects upon them a crimson flood which, to the pious natives, is as the blood of Christ. Some of the early Indians called the Rockies "The Shining Mountains."

Our return brought us back to Five Points at four-thirty o'clock. Dismounting, I threw my arms around Buck's neck and thanked him by saying: "Good old Buck!" while patting him affectionately.

Buck took it like a man but, looking up, I discovered that Red had witnessed the incident and was eyeing me with more expression than he had shown all day—surprise, mixed perhaps with faint approval and a little amusement. I experienced the usual embarrassment of a man caught in a sentimental act. I have, in this freedom, been saving my inhibitions for a later day. Now, I perceive, my time is about up.

The boys were more tired than they have been on any of our other projects but, with baths and a rest, they reported to supper refreshed. Buttons, walking with an unfamiliar gait, was asked where he got it.

"He paid a dollar and a half for it!" retorted Art, quoting the price of a horse for the day.

As our horses climbed the mountains, frequently the gap between mounts widened until one rode in solitude. This was the best of the day ... to ride alone, singing, thinking, and looking. One thought struck deeper than the rest: that the days we have spent here have been lived upon the verge of poetry, not poetry in words, but poetry felt and lived within the unexplored depths of the spirit.

The Nineteenth Chapter

I am the wanderer. My contentment is to
*   annihilate distances;*
Never again will I be satisfied with
*   a quatrain of horizons.*
I salute only the undiscovered and the
*   unexplored.*
Adventure is for me and for those who will
*   not be caged by dead yesterdays.*

Thursday, September 4

WEATHER: Fair. Temperature at 5:30 A.M. 50° F.

CONDITION of Party: On the move.

As the sun struck the halfway point on the western range of mountains, yet not high enough to penetrate the depths of Five Points Canyon, we assembled at the Lodge for breakfast, our last meal at Philmont.

It was six-fifteen, and Billy had everything ready and waiting. He apologized for not having sour-dough biscuits, explaining that he was not very successful at cooking them indoors where he could not use his Dutch oven.

We said good-by to our friends, Billy waving his new hat, and within the hour were on our way to Cimarron, Eagle's Nest, Raton, Taos, and Sante Fe.

The drive through Cimarron Canyon was bright and crisp, the air a tonic. Any medicine man might do his lazy braves a service by prescribing some hours of this air breathed deeply for purification, but well away from the dust of Highway No. 64.

Eagle's Nest Lake, choppy and blue, with the Sangre de Cristo Mountains in the background, was a rare sight in New Mexico, where lakes are phenomena. It would be just another pond in Maine, but here it commands exclamations of respect.

Taos, picturesque and ancient, merited a four-hour

142

stop and the party went on a spending spree, the glittering hand-wrought silver and turquoise handiwork of the Indians proving irresistible in the thought of loved ones at home. Irv and I bought beautiful Navajo rugs.

"This place," said Buttons, "has a distinct atmosphere of its own. The people are truly characters of description."

We liked the adobe architecture of Taos, but the jacal construction of the poor, more typical of the open country, seemed boxlike and curious. These homes are constructed of mud over a wooden frame, and the grass grows on their dirt roofs. Sometimes, on hot nights, the natives sleep there under the stars. In one case a goat was placidly grazing on top!

We left the main highway to visit San Juan Pueblo, an Indian reservation of the Tesque. Here we purchased, at reasonable prices, fine specimens of their ceramics. The swarming children gave the lie to an old phrase about "the vanishing red man," and suggested a more appropriate one: "the replenishing red man." It is a fact that the Indians are actually gaining in numbers at a rate faster than that of the white population of the United States today.

One of the Indians invited me inside his home to look at some handiwork and I was agreeably surprised at the cleanliness and taste of the home arrangement. I commented on this to Irv, who replied that he did not see how the home could be so neat when the children were so dirty.

A little girl of about ten years and several smaller children surrounded me, with importunities to purchase a small vase.

"Fifteen cents! Fifteen cents! Fifteen cents!" she chanted, holding the vessel up in front of my face.

"No, I do not want the vase," I replied, "but what is this little boy's name?" pointing to a cunning little four-year-old with straight dark hair, black eyes, dirty face, and running nose.

"My brother, Louis," she replied, without changing her tone, "fifteen cents! fifteen cents!"

"Good!" I exclaimed. "I'll take him. Come along, Louis."

"No! No!" she shouted, holding up the vase again. "This for fifteen cents!"

"I'll give you half a dollar for Louis."

"No! No! No!" she protested, shaking her head violently and pushing little Louis behind her. "The pot, the pot, the pot, for fifteen cents."

"Well," I continued to negotiate, "I'll give you this dollar for Louis." I took the large silver coin from my pocket and held it up for all to see.

"No," she said, again shaking her head, but with less emphasis.

Meanwhile, Louis appeared to be hugely enjoying this haggling, his wide black eyes shining as he looked eagerly from me to his sister. He would not stay behind her but jumped up and down excitedly between us.

Deliberately I took another silver dollar from my pocket and clinked the two together.

"Two dollars for little Louis!" I announced with an air of the utmost extravagance. The children gasped.

The little girl looked at the two bright coins as they flashed in the sun, and her lips parted in indecision. One of the other children gave her a faint nod of encouragement. Little Louis, sensing the crisis, went suddenly sober.

"You wait," said the little girl, "until I get his hat."

"No," I answered, "I've decided to take the vase instead."

I parted with more than the fifteen cents, and pressed an extra coin into little Louis' chubby hand. Surveying their treasures, the children turned and ran like rabbits to their home pueblos.

They had known, all along, that it was just a game.

We visited the little mission church, and I did not know until later why Buttons had hesitated to go in. He explained in his diary:

"Chief persuaded us to go into the Indian Church. I didn't want to at first because I thought they might want to fulfill the purpose of the church, to convert people, and I hate to take chances. However, I decided my fears were groundless and went in. I was surprised at the inside. It was beautiful."

We arrived at Santa Fe at five o'clock and settled for the night in one of the swank tourists camps which are typical of this part of the West. These camps incline toward the gaudy, but vie with each other in conveniences for the traveler. Ours included a tennis court.

From campers to sophisticated travelers, we had made the transition complete within the day. At evening we strode before the historic long Palace of the Governors like common tourists, while all about the air hung heavy with the overwhelming weight of history. But we ourselves felt no weight. Our labors for the time were over, and we paraded the streets of Santa Fe in the satisfied manner of strangers showing off in distant places.

The Twentieth Chapter

Men write their histories with blinded eyes,
Naming generals, kings, and presidents
   As greater than the genuinely wise.

Yet, only those are great who serve mankind,
With humble skills and careful science,
   Extending the horizons of the mind.

Tomorrow we will write an honest page
In praise of scholars and of noble men,
   With footnotes for generals in that age.

Friday, September 5

CONDITION of Party: On good behavior.

We spent the morning at the Laboratory of Anthropology. This institution stands as a kind of cultural oasis in the midst of the problems it is intended to study. It is about two miles south of the Plaza and is of distinctive adobe architecture. Within is a well-ordered atmosphere of authoritative science. The priceless exhibits of pottery, textiles, basketry, silver, and other Indian arts have been arranged with masterful effect.

As is true of most scientific institutions, some of the more important aspects did not meet the eye. Laboratories, workrooms, and storage areas are usually located in the basements and isolated wings of such institutions, far away from the distractions of the exhibition halls. In them the scientists and the technicians perform the tasks which make possible the pretentious halls above and are seldom, if ever, dissatisfied with their cubbyholes, having learned, long since, that in the eyes of the public a specimen is entitled to better quarters than a man.

I had had preliminary correspondence with our host, Dr. H. P. Mera, and judging from his letters had visualized him as a young man of thirty-five or so. We found him in his laboratory surounded by color charts, besmoked and busy. He was gray-bearded, dignified,

148

and scholarly, with genial eyes and a deep warm voice. Shoving aside his work he appraised our materials, section by section, as Bob and Art took careful notes. He would, he agreed, have our tree-ring specimens dated for us. He guessed they would fall between 1000 and 1100 A.D., as the remainder of our material is consistently early Pueblo, possibly Second Period Chaco.

Dr. Mera's unassuming sincerity touched me, and when he reminded us that a visit to him prior to our excavations might have enabled us better to anticipate some of our problems, I recognized the mistake and regretted it. Actually we had expected that he might visit our project at Philmont, but he had been unable to do so. His achievements are well known in archaeology.

We have always had a distorted sense of history in that we hold our professional soldiers and politicians in greater regard than our scientists and scholars. No doubt we help to breed future wars by overacclaimation of our generals and the deification of "war presidents." Some histories will give a tobacco-chewing general half a dozen chapters while Emerson and Thoreau get scarcely a line.

I wanted to make some small purchases for the members of my family and searched the stores for something for a boy. There were baubles of all sorts to delight the heart of a girl, but only the conventional things for boys that can be purchased from Portland to Los Angeles. I explained my problem to one of the clerks, who attempted to persuade me to buy a bracelet for my young son.

"But boys do not wear bracelets," I protested.

"Oh, yes, they do," she replied, "indeed they do in Sante Fe."

But Hamden, Connecticut, is different, I told her, compromising on a small turquoise ring.

Our host recommended a restaurant famous for its Mexican cooking. He said that Duncan Hines, the author of *Adventures in Good Eating*, the tourist guide for professional gadabouts, had given it a good rating. In the mood for a change of fare, I decided to try it and Buttons agreed to accompany me. It was an adventure! The Mexican dishes were fiery enough to put one in trim for the nether regions, and it took Buttons five glasses of water to wash his down.

"If Duncan Hines," he said, practically breathing fire, " has eaten in all the places he says he has, I'll bet he is overweight and has a cast-iron stomach to boot."

During the evening we were visited by a hospitable young scout leader of Santa Fe.

"Do you expect any of the boys to become archaeologists as a result of your expedition?" he asked.

"I don't think so," I answered.

"Then what purpose did your expedition accomplish so far as the boys are concerned?"

I smiled that I should be called upon to defend our trip.

"The adventure might be enough," I suggested.

"But you could have had adventure without going to so much trouble."

"Yes," I replied, "but I wished it to be an adventure of the mind as well as the body."

"Did you accomplish that?"

"Yes, at least that much. If my boys have nothing

else, they have gained an appreciation of the scientific method which should stand them in good stead no matter what they do."

"What is the scientific method?"

I squirmed. How could one explain in a few words the exacting demands of scientific method and experiment? Besides, I did not think that even this was the full measure of the worth of our expedition. I turned to Bob, who had been working with his notebook near by.

"Bob," I called, "what is the scientific method?"

"The scientific method? Let me see. That is a tough one. I guess it's being careful enough to get the facts instead of the suppositions."

"Naturally," I added, "the steps will not be the same in different fields. But don't you think Bob is close enough?"

"Yes, I do," he replied. And after a moment, "I wish I had been along."

Overcome by this compliment, I passed him my field notes to read. He took a glance at them, turned a few pages apprehensively, and remembered an urgent appointment.

Bob laughed.

"If you want to get rid of anyone, Chief, just hand them your journal."

"All right," I replied, "you take it and read it for a while."

The Last Chapter

I will be proud when the day is over,
  And will return to the Earth, my mother,
Bearing the small garlands of my journey
  To start me outward on another.

$\mathcal{S}$aturday, September 6

WEATHER: Fair. Temperature at 7 A.M. 60° F.

CONDITION of Party: Rested.

Turning to Button's diary for the last time, we start our day:

"This morning I took an extra special shower for who knows where we may be sleeping tonight, under the stars, with the rattlesnakes, or even in a hotel. I wasn't alone for, in a short time, a barber shop chorus arose to disturb the peaceful neighbors. We were a well scrubbed crew that stepped out into the early Santa Fe air.

"Packing the station wagon we rode down to the Faith Cafe. People were hurrying to their places of business, brightly dressed Indians were scurrying to the market with their wares, merchants could be seen unlocking the doors of their establishments, and now and then a highly polished stenographer tripping down the street. All of this tended to increase our excitement."

We had fruit juice and pancakes, and I paid the check. Yesterday, in order to avoid placing restrictions on liberty, I issued each boy a dollar and twenty-five cents with instructions to purchase his own food during the day. When evening came I found that the regular procedure had been to eat hamburgers and drink sodas. One had eaten three meals on sixty cents, spending his "earnings" on souvenirs.

In addition to being custodian of the expedition's

154

funds, I am banker for the boys. They began the trip with an average of over twenty dollars apiece on deposit in what we call the First Rational Bank. We use actual check blanks (from a depression-defunct irrational bank) which the boys fill out in the amounts needed and which I cash, keeping the check as record and receipt. The system works perfectly and, since the boys' signatures show for every withdrawal, there is never a question involving the accuracy of the accounts. Each boy also has a page in our small Budget Book from which his financial status can be given in a matter of seconds. I carry a nominal amount of cash, keeping the bulk of our funds in travelers' checks.

Our expedition is budgeted as follows:

Transportation and Insurance	$320.
Food and Accommodations (Includes Billy's employment)	400.
Equipment and small supplies (First aid, etc.)	20.
Scientific Expense (Tools and working materials)	30.
Express and Cartage	30.
Reserve for Emergencies and for Unanticipated Expenses	100.
Total	$900.

We think our costs are moderate in the light of the values we are receiving. Our budget includes thirty-one days' maintenance and five thousand miles' travel. We are comfortably on schedule, financially, and expect to balance out at the end of the trip.

We reached our station wagon just ahead of a policeman with his parking tickets, not knowing whether we could trust his softness of heart. A friendly officer in another city fed his own pennies to the parking meter in order to avoid ticketing our scout car. He had a son, he told me, who was a First Class scout. He would not let me refund his pennies. I should have taken his Irish name, for I am sure he will be elevated to the sainthood some day and, if he is on traffic duty at St. Peter's gates, many a sinner will get an unexpected green light.

Santa Fe, according to our guidebook, is the oldest seat of government in the United States. The Indians had a settlement here long before any white man ever saw it, perhaps for a century or two, perhaps for a thousand years. First it was an Indian pueblo, then a Spanish capital, then an Indian city again, Spanish once more, then Mexican, and finally American. The ancient Pueblos called it "the dancing ground of the sun."

As we drove by the Palace of the Governors, the Indians were already assembling with their wares in keeping with their Saturday custom. They brought their goods wrapped in brilliant blankets thrown over their shoulders, and displayed them by spreading the blankets out on the wide porch, arranging the articles upon them, and then sitting, pipe serene, behind. Necklaces, bracelets, rings, and brooches of silver and turquoise; vases, baskets, and serapes; red, yellow, and freckled ears of corn, and bright woolen goods were there.

A squaw sprawled her little papoose among her baubles and changed his diaper while he scowled at a fly on his nose. The characters change, but life goes on in front of the Palace of the Governors.

We stopped to enter the Cathedral of St. Francis of Assisi. Here the archbishop of whom Willa Cather wrote lies buried beneath the altar of the noble church he built. It was by accident, I thought, rather than by design, that we came to the cathedral as our last act before turning homeward. Art might see a purpose in it. None of us would deny its inspiration and beauty.

Small reverent sounds punctuated the cathedral quietness, hardly more than the soft footsteps and faint rustlings of arriving and departing worshipers with their discreet coughings. The mellow sunlight filtered through the stained-glass windows while the candles burned in yellow points of flame. The setting was for thoughts of God, and mine were all of man.

Homo sapiens, the thinking animal, might be a million years old as a species. (That is not really long. A million years is a breath of universal time.) But if man has come a long way, he has a longer way to go.

He might take comfort, and a little pride, in his growth. There was a time when to be savage was his nature. In that age he was hunter by instinct and he killed, or took what he wanted, without any sense of guilt or remorse. His highest morality was to survive, selfishness was his nature, and expediency his rule of thumb. It was an Age of Simplicity in which he did not see beyond his own animal needs.

When he found that he could use his wits to supplement his strength, his next great period dawned in the Age of Barbarism. He became a social creature, organizing tribes and nations. He learned to trade, and acquired a certain mastery of the land from which he developed his present culture, based upon agriculture and the use of metals. He became clever at invention.

But he was and is still a barbarian, organizing his killings, and turning his primitive instincts against himself.

And whither? Shall it be, at last, to an Age of Understanding? It took a million years for him to outgrow his Age of Simplicity and he has been a barbarian only a little while. The centuries must roll. Yet, in the end, I believe his Age of Understanding will arrive.

For every error man can find a greater truth, for every weakness a greater strength, and for every misery a deeper joy.

Cathedrals of stone cannot be higher or more beautiful than his thoughts. What man has created, he can surpass. What he can conceive, he may hope to achieve. Time, his master, may also be his slave. He has only to use it well. Not for a year, merely; not for a generation only; but if there is a forever, then it must be forever.

Leaving the cathedral, we turned the Quinnipiac Scouter homeward in silence, until Wally cried out at the next bend:

"Look! The route number! Good old Sixty-four! The way home!"

When I have tried to tell the best, I have failed ... the words floating like dry leaves upon a river of the unspoken. Somewhere, in my mind, flowing deeper than words, a new stream of memory has joined its course with the treasured visions of the past; Wally and Buttons raising the flag of their wide America; Irv, with the rain in his face, and the gleam in his eye; Art with his prayer book, seeking worship in the quiet glen; and Bob emerging, blissfully unwashed, from the cold river. I see Tops again, with his coat of many colors; Billy, the cowboy, talking to his horses; and Rodney, the beloved scholar, disappearing over the high mountain.

I have had more than I deserve, and if *Papilio perturbans* comes again, in some sharp moment which may be, indeed, my last, I shall laugh with the Earth, my mother, knowing that she has never deprived me, but having made me her child, and indulged me for a while, is ready now to weave me, with my friends of long ago, into the eternal garment of her ageless dust.

CPSIA information can be obtained
at www.ICGtesting.com
Printed in the USA
BVHW041425280821
615439BV00001B/64